easy fair isle knitting

27 projects with a modern twist

Martin Storey

Photography by Steven Wooster

TS

TRAFALGAR SQUARE
North Pomfret, Vermont

Easy Fair Isle Knitting
First published in the United States of America
In 2016 by
Trafalgar Square Books
North Pomfret, Vermont 05053

The instructions and material lists in this book were
carefully reviewed by the author and editor; however, accuracy
cannot be guaranteed. The author and publisher cannot be held
liable for errors.

ISBN: 978-1-57076-785-2
Library of Congress Control Number: 2016935523

Designer: Anne Wilson
Editor: Katie Hardwicke
Pattern writer (and knitting): Penny Hill
Pattern checker: Jill Gray
Charts: Anne Wilson
Stylist: Susan Berry
Special photography (pages 7, 126-7, 128,
and back cover): Hazel Young

Printed in China
10 9 8 7 6 5 4 3 2 1

contents

introduction

When I was asked to create the designs for a book of patterns that made Fair Isle both simple and contemporary, I jumped at the chance, because I love to work with color and particularly enjoy the intricate but subtle effect you get when knitting with two colors in a row. In fact, I had fairly recently returned from a wonderful workshop in the Shetland Islands, which gave me lots of inspiration for this book.

Lots of people love the look of Fair Isle patterns but assume it will be difficult to knit them. That is certainly true of some of the exquisite traditional Fair Isle sweaters with lots of color changes, but even a novice knitter would not find the patterns in this book hard to knit for three reasons: firstly the designs I have included are generally small; secondly the majority have no shaping (which can be harder to work in Fair Isle); and thirdly they only employ two colors in a row, which is not hard to handle even for a novice knitter.

I have included quite a few pillows in the book, in part because I think the Fair Isle patterns are a great addition to an otherwise plain couch or chair, and also because once you get into the groove, they are very easy to work. You can then put several different patterned pillows together to great effect. The scarves are similarly easy to knit. Even the bag is not difficult because the Fair Isle pattern is worked on a straight piece of knitting.

The socks, hats, and vests are a little more complicated but not much, because the Fair Isle element is kept pretty simple and there is very little shaping to do at the points when the more complicated Fair Isle pattern is involved. As an extra bit of fun, I have included a Nordic tree design for a pillow, throw, and garland. The latter could be knitted quite easily even by a child!

I hope you have as much fun knitting the designs as I did creating them.

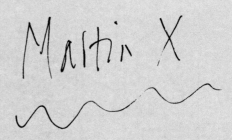

fair isle knits for you and your home

heart wave scarf

little rabbits scarf and hat

little circles scarf

kitten and stripe scarf

tree and ripple bag

waves vest

little hearts vest

 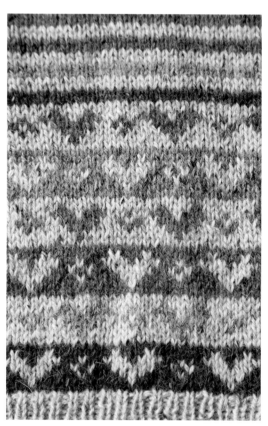

little hearts cowl

little owls cowl

folk cowl

folk warmer

EASY FAIR ISLE KNITTING

31

plaid
and
diamond
socks

EASY FAIR ISLE KNITTING

plaid and diamond beanie

soft stripe gloves...

...and soft stripe beret

EASY FAIR ISLE KNITTING

little circles pillow

paper dolls pillow

simple
spots
pillow

EASY FAIR ISLE KNITTING

paper boats pillow

goosey pillow

nordic pillow

nordic garland

nordic throw

counting sheep throw

little houses tablet and i-phone cover

the patterns

little rabbits scarf

FINISHED SIZE
4¼in/11cm wide by 69½in/176cm long
(excluding pompoms)

YARN
Rowan *Felted Tweed*
2 x 1¾oz/191yd balls in Clay 177 (A)
1 x 1¾oz/191yd ball in each of Avocado 161
(B), Peony 183 (C), and Watery 152 (D)

NEEDLES
Pair of size 5 (3.75mm) knitting needles
1 spare needle for bind off

GAUGE
23 sts and 28 rows to 4in/10cm square over
patterned St st using size 5 (3.75mm)
needles, or size to obtain correct gauge.

ABBREVIATIONS
See page 127.

NOTE
When working from chart, right side rows
are knit rows and read from right to left.
Wrong side rows are purl rows and read
from left to right.
Use the Fair Isle method: strand the yarns
not in use across the wrong side of work,
weaving them under and over the working
yarn every 3 or 4 sts.

TO MAKE
FIRST SIDE
Using size 5 (3.75mm) needles and A,
cast on 16 sts.
Row 1 (WS) P to end.
Row 2 K1, [m1, k1] 13 times, m1, k2.
30 sts.
Row 3 P to end.
Row 4 K2, [m1, k1] 25 times, m1, k3.
56 sts.
Work in patt.
Row 5 P to end.
Row 6 K[1A, 1B] to end.
Row 7 P1A, 1B, [3A, 1B] to end.
Row 8 As row 6.
Row 9 Using A, p to end.
Work in patt from Chart A.
Row 10 K1A, [work across 9-st patt rep]
6 times, k1A.
Row 11 P1A, [work across 9-st patt rep]
6 times, p1A.
These 2 rows set Chart A with one st in
St st using A at sides.
Work in patt to end of row 10.
Rows 20 to 24 As rows 5 to 9.
Work in patt from Chart B.
Row 25 K1A, [work across 9-st patt rep]
6 times, k1A.
Row 26 P1A, [work across 9-st patt rep]
6 times, p1A.
These 2 rows set Chart B with one st in

CHART A

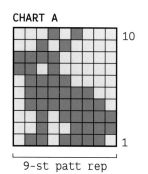

9-st patt rep

CHART B

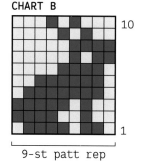

9-st patt rep

KEY

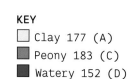
☐ Clay 177 (A)
▨ Peony 183 (C)
■ Watery 152 (D)

St st using A at sides.
Work in patt to end of
row 10.
Rows 5 to 34 form the
patt.
Cont in patt until first
half measures approx
35½in/90cm, ending with
row 34.
Leave sts on a spare
needle.

SECOND SIDE
Work to match first side
until piece measures
approx 34in/86cm, ending
with row 23.

FINISHING
With needles pointing in
the same direction and
right sides together,
using A, bind off the sts
of both pieces together.
Join row ends of scarf
together.
Run a thread through cast-
on sts, pull up tightly,
and secure.
Join row ends together.
Using B, make 2 pompoms
and attach one to each
end.

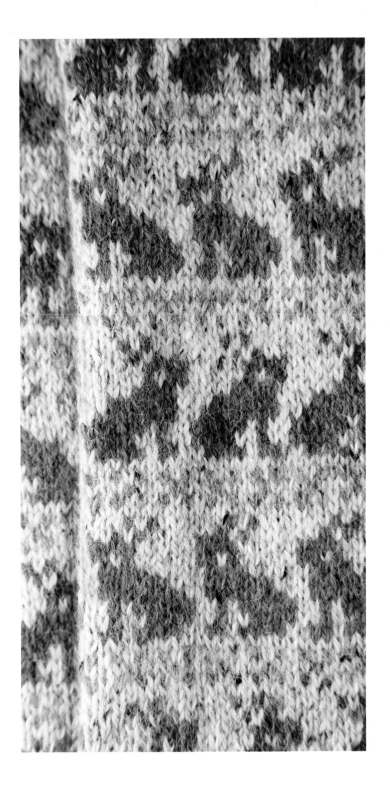

little rabbits hat

FINISHED SIZE
To fit child age 3–7 years

YARN
Rowan *Felted Tweed*
1 x 1¾oz/191yd ball in each of Clay 177 (A), Avocado 161 (B), Peony 183 (C), and Watery 152 (D)

NEEDLES
Pair each of size 3 (3.25mm) and size 5 (3.75mm) knitting needles

GAUGE
23 sts and 28 rows to 4in/10cm square over patterned St st using size 5 (3.75mm) needles, or size to obtain correct gauge.

ABBREVIATIONS
See page 127.

NOTE
When working from chart, right side rows are knit rows and read from right to left. Wrong side rows are purl rows and read from left to right.

Use the Fair Isle method: strand the yarns not in use across the wrong side of work, weaving them under and over the working yarn every 3 or 4 sts.

TO MAKE
Using size 3 (3.25mm) needles and A, cast on 110 sts.
Row 1 P2, [k2, p2] to end.
Row 2 K2, [p2, k2] to end.
These 2 rows form the rib.
Work a further 9 rows.
Row 12 P to end.
Change to size 5 (3.75mm) needles.
Work in patt.
Row 1 K[1A, 1B] to end.
Row 2 P1A, 1B, [3A, 1B] to end.
Row 3 As row 1.
Row 4 Using A, p to end.
Work in patt from Chart A.
Row 5 K1A, [work across 9-st patt rep] 12 times, k1A.
Row 6 P1A, [work across 9-st patt rep] 12 times, p1A.
These 2 rows set Chart A with one st in St st using A at sides.
Work in patt to end of row 10.
Row 15 Using A, k to end.
Row 16 P[1B, 1A] to end.
Row 17 K[1B,3A] to last 2 sts, 1B, 1A.
Row 18 As row 16.
Row 19 Using A, k to end.
Work in patt from Chart B.
Row 20 P1A, [work across 9-st patt rep] 12 times, k1A.
Row 21 K1A, [work across 9-st patt rep]

CHART A

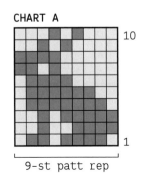

10

1

9-st patt rep

CHART B

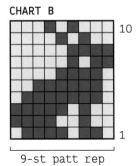

10

1

9-st patt rep

KEY
☐ Clay 177 (A)
▨ Peony 183 (C)
◼ Watery 152 (D)

12 times, p1A.

These 2 rows set Chart B with one st in St st using A at sides.

Work in patt to end of row 10.

Row 30 Using A, p to end.

Rows 31 to 34 As rows 1 to 4.

Cont in A only.

Work 6 rows, inc one st at center of row. *111 sts.*

SHAPE CROWN

Row 1 [K9, k2tog] 10 times, k1. *101 sts.*

Row 2 and every WS row P to end.

Row 3 [K8, k2tog] 10 times, k1. *91 sts.*

Row 5 [K7, k2tog] 10 times, k1. *81 sts.*

Row 7 [K6, k2tog] 10 times, k1. *71 sts.*

Row 9 [K5, k2tog] 10 times, k1. *61 sts.*

Row 11 [K4, k2tog] 10 times, k1. *51 sts.*

Row 13 [K3, k2tog] 10 times, k1. *41 sts.*

Row 15 [K2, k2tog] 10 times, k1. *31 sts.*

Row 17 [K1, k2tog] 10 times, k1. *21 sts.*

Row 19 [K2tog] 10 times, k1. *11 sts.*

Row 20 P to end.

Break off yarn, thread yarn through rem sts, pull up tightly, and fasten off securely.

FINISHING

Join back seam. Using B, make a pompom and attach to top of hat.

little circles scarf

FINISHED SIZE
One size: 6in/15cm wide by 43¼in/110cm long

YARN
Rowan *Felted Tweed*
3 x 1¾oz/191yd balls in Celadon 184 (A)
1 x 1¾oz/191yd ball in each of Tawny 186 (B) and Mineral 181 (C)

NEEDLES
Pair each of size 3 (3.25mm) and size 5 (3.75mm) needles

GAUGE
23 sts and 32 rows to 4in/10cm square over St st using size 5 (3.75mm) needles, or size to obtain correct gauge.

ABBREVIATIONS
See page 127.

NOTE
When working from chart, odd numbered rows are knit rows and read from right to left. Even numbered rows are purl rows and read from left to right.
Use the Fair Isle method: strand the yarns not in use across the wrong side of work, weaving them under and over the working yarn every 3 or 4 sts.

TO MAKE (make 2 pieces)
Using size 5 (3.75mm) needles and A, cast on 72 sts.
Beg with a k row, work in St st and patt from Chart.
Row 1 Using A, k to end.
Row 2 Using A, p to end.
Row 3 Work one st before patt rep, [work across 5-st patt rep] 14 times, work one st after patt rep.
Row 4 Work one st before patt rep, [work across 5-st patt rep] 14 times, work one st after patt rep.
Rows 3 and 4 set the Chart.
Work in patt to end of row 12.
Rows 13 to 23 Rep rows 3 to 12 once, and row 3 again.
Row 24 Using A, p to end.
Row 25 Using A, k to end.
Row 26 P2A, P[1C, 3A] to last 2 sts, 1C, 1A.
Row 27 Using A, k to end.
Row 28 Using A, p to end.
Row 29 K[3A, 1C] to end.
Rows 24 to 29 form the spot patt.
Cont in spot patt until piece measures 21¾in/55cm, ending with a plain row.
Leave sts on a spare needle.

FINISHING
With needles pointing in the same direction, right sides together, using A bind off the sts of both pieces together.
Join row ends of scarf together.
With seam running down center of scarf, using size 3 (3.25mm) needles and C, working through both thicknesses, pick up and k24 sts along one short end.
K 2 rows.
Bind off.
Work other end to match.

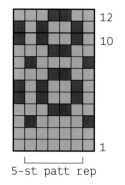

5-st patt rep

KEY
Celadon 184 (A)
Tawny 186 (B)

kitten and stripe scarf

FINISHED SIZE
One size: approx 4¾in/11cm wide by
75in/190cm long

YARN
Rowan *Felted Tweed*
2 x 1¾oz/191yd balls in Scree 165 (A)
1 x 1¾oz/191yd ball in each of Bilberry
151 (B), Avocado 161 (C), Ginger 154 (D),
and Watery 152 (E)

NEEDLES
Pair each of size 3 (3.25mm) and size 5
(3.75mm) needles

GAUGE
23 sts and 32 rows to 4in/10cm square
over St st using size 5 (3.75mm) needles,
or size to obtain correct gauge.

ABBREVIATIONS
See page 127.

NOTE
When working from chart, odd numbered
rows are knit rows and read from right
to left. Even numbered rows are purl rows
and read from left to right.
Use the Fair isle method: strand the
yarns not in use across the wrong side
of work, weaving them under and over the
working yarn every 3 or 4 sts.

TO MAKE (make 2 pieces)
FIRST PIECE
Using size 3 (3.25mm) needles and B,
cast on 58 sts.
Beg with a k row, work in St st and
stripes of 2 rows each B, A, C, A, D, A,
E, A.
Change to size 5 (3.75mm) needles.
Work in patt from Chart.
Row 1 K2A, [work across 7-st patt rep]
8 times.

Row 2 [Work across 7-st patt rep]
8 times, p2A.
These 2 rows set Chart.
Work in patt to end of row 28.
Rep these 28 rows 7 times more, and rows
1 to 27 once more.
Leave sts on a spare needle.
SECOND PIECE
Using size 3 (3.25mm) needles and B,
cast on 58 sts.

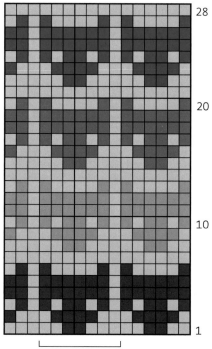

7-st patt rep

KEY
⬜ Scree 165 (A)
⬛ Bilberry 151 (B)
⬜ Avocado 161 (C)
⬛ Ginger 154 (D)
⬛ Watery 152 (E)

Beg with a k row, work in
St st and stripes of
2 rows each B, A, C, A, D,
A, E, A.
Change to size 5 (3.75mm)
needles.
Work in patt from Chart.
Row 1 K1A, [work across
7-st patt rep] 7 times,
k1A.
Row 2 P1A, [work across
7-st patt rep] 7 times,
p1A.
These 2 rows set Chart.
Work in patt to end of
row 28.
Rep these 28 rows 7 times
more, and rows 1 to 20
again.
Leave sts on a spare
needle.

FINISHING

With needles pointing in
the same direction, right
sides together, using A
bind off the sts of both
pieces together.
Join row ends of scarf
together.
Join bound-off edge and
cast-on edge to form a
tube.

heart wave scarf

FINISHED SIZE
6in/15cm wide by 82½in/210cm long
(excluding pompoms)

YARN
Rowan *Felted Tweed*
2 x 1¾oz/191yd balls in each of Rage 150
(A), Mineral 181 (B), Pine 158 (C), and
Duck Egg 173 (D)

NEEDLES
Pair of size 5 (3.75mm) knitting needles
1 spare needle for bind off

GAUGE
23 sts and 28 rows to 4in/10cm square
over patterned St st using size 5
(3.75mm) needles, or size to obtain
correct gauge.

ABBREVIATIONS
See page 127.

NOTE
When working from chart, right side rows
are knit rows and read from right to
left. Wrong side rows are purl rows and
read from left to right.
Use the Fair Isle method: strand the
yarns not in use across the wrong side
of work, weaving them under and over the
working yarn every 3 or 4 sts.

TO MAKE
FIRST SIDE
Using size 5 (3.75mm) needles and A,
cast on 20 sts.
Row 1 (WS) P to end.
Row 2 K1, [m1, k1] 17 times, m1, k2.
38 sts.
Row 3 P to end.
Row 4 K2, [m1, k1] 33 times, m1, k3. *72 sts.*
Row 5 P to end.
Work in patt from Chart A.
Row 1 Using A, work to end.
Row 2 Using A, work to end.
Row 3 Work one st before patt rep,
[work across 10-st patt rep] 7 times,
work one st after patt rep.
Row 4 Work one st before patt rep,
[work across 10-st patt rep] 7 times,
work one st after patt rep.
Rows 3 and 4 set Chart A.
Work in patt to end of row 11.
Work 2 rows C, 2 rows B, 1 row D.
Row 17 (inc row) Using D, k18, m1, k36,
m1, k18. *74 sts.*
Work in patt from Chart B.
Row 18 Work one st before patt rep,
[work across 6-st patt rep] 12 times,
work one st after patt rep.
Row 19 Work one st before patt rep,
[work across 6-st patt rep] 12 times,
work one st after patt rep.
Row 20 Work one st before patt rep,
[work across 6-st patt rep] 12 times,
work one st after patt rep.
Row 21 (dec row) Using C, k18, k2tog, k34,
k2tog, k18. *72 sts.*
Row 22 Using C, work to end.
Work in patt from Chart C.
Row 23 Work one st before patt rep,
[work across 5-st patt rep] 14 times,
work one st after patt rep.
Row 24 Work one st before patt rep,
[work across 5-st patt rep] 14 times,
work one st after patt rep.

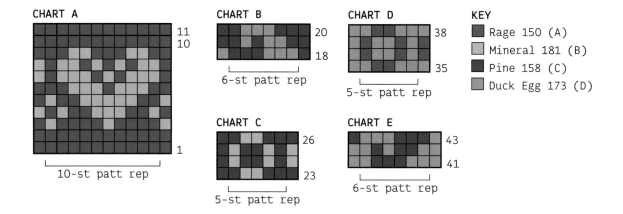

CHART A

11
10

1

10-st patt rep

CHART B

20

18

6-st patt rep

CHART C

26

23

5-st patt rep

CHART D

38

35

5-st patt rep

CHART E

43

41

6-st patt rep

KEY
- Rage 150 (A)
- Mineral 181 (B)
- Pine 158 (C)
- Duck Egg 173 (D)

Row 25 Work one st before patt rep,
[work across 5-st patt rep] 14 times,
work one st after patt rep.
Row 26 Work one st before patt rep,
[work across 5-st patt rep] 14 times,
work one st after patt rep.
Work 2 rows C, 2 rows D, 2 rows A,
2 rows D.
Work in patt from Chart D.
Row 35 Work one st before patt rep,
[work across 5-st patt rep] 14 times,
work one st after patt rep.
Row 36 Work one st before patt rep,
[work across 5-st patt rep] 14 times,
work one st after patt rep.
Row 37 Work one st before patt rep,
[work across 5-st patt rep] 14 times,
work one st after patt rep.
Row 38 Work one st before patt rep,
[work across 5-st patt rep] 14 times,
work one st after patt rep.
Work 1 row D.
Row 40 (inc row) Using D, p18, m1, p36,
m1, p18. *74 sts.*
Work in patt from Chart E.
Row 41 Work one st before patt rep,
[work across 6-st patt rep] 12 times,
work one st after patt rep.
Row 42 Work one st before patt rep,
[work across 6-st patt rep] 12 times,
work one st after patt rep.

Row 43 Work one st before patt rep,
[work across 6-st patt rep] 12 times,
work one st after patt rep.
Row 44 (dec row) Using C, p18, p2tog,
p34, p2tog, p18. *72 sts.*
Row 45 Using C, work to end.
Work 2 rows B and 2 rows D.
These 49 rows form the patt.
Noting that inc and dec rows will
alternate between k rows and p rows, work
a further 244 rows, ending with a 48th
row of patt.
Leave sts on a spare needle.
SECOND SIDE
Work to match first side.

FINISHING
With needles pointing in the same
direction and right sides together,
using D bind off the sts of both pieces
together.
Join row ends of scarf together.
Run a thread through cast-on sts, pull
up tightly, and secure. Join row ends
together.
Using A, make 2 pompoms and attach one to
each end.

tree and ripple bag

FINISHED SIZE
Approx 11¾in/30cm wide by 12½in/32cm deep

YARN
Rowan *Felted Tweed*
2 x 1¾oz/191yd balls in Clay 177 (A)
1 x 1¾oz/191yd ball in each of Gilt 160
(B), Celadon 184 (C), Damask 182 (D), and
Maritime 167 (E)

NEEDLES
Pair each of size 3 (3.25mm) and size 5
(3.75mm) knitting needles
Size 3 (3.25mm) circular needle
Stitch holders

EXTRAS
39in/100cm of 1in/2.5cm wide grosgrain
ribbon

GAUGE
26 sts and 26 rows to 4in/10cm square
patterned St st using size 5 (3.75mm)
needles, or size to obtain correct gauge.

ABBREVIATIONS
See page 127.

NOTE
When working from chart, odd numbered
rows are knit rows and read from right
to left. Even numbered rows are purl rows
and read from left to right.
Use the Fair Isle method: strand the
yarns not in use across the wrong side
of work, weaving them under and over the
working yarn every 3 or 4 sts.

BAG

BACK AND FRONT (alike)
Using size 5 (3.75mm) needles and A,
cast on 73 sts.
Work in patt from Chart A.
Row 1 [Work across 12-st patt rep]
6 times, then work last st of Chart.
Row 2 Work first st of Chart, then [work
across 12-st patt rep] 6 times.
These 2 rows set the Chart.
Work in patt from Chart to end of row 20.
Next row K to end, inc one st at center
of row. *74 sts.*
Work in patt from Chart B.
Row 1 Work one st before patt rep,
[work across 6-st patt rep] 12 times,
then work one st after patt.
Row 2 Work one st before patt rep,
[work across 6-st patt rep] 12 times,
then work one st after patt.
These 2 rows set the Chart.
Cont in patt to end of row 16, then rep
rows 1 to 16 until piece measures approx
12in/30cm, ending on a p row in A.
Leave these sts on a holder.

GUSSET (make 2)
Using size 5 (3.75mm) needles and A,
cast on 19 sts.
Beg with a k row, work in St st until
piece fits from halfway across cast-on
edge, ending with a p row, inc one st at
end of last row.
Mark each end of last row with a colored
thread.
Work in patt from Chart C.
Row 1 K2A, work across 15 sts of Chart C,
k2A.
Row 2 P2A, work across 15 sts of Chart C,
p2A.
These 2 rows set the Chart.
Work in patt from Chart to end of row 20.
Next row K to end, inc one st at center
of row. *20 sts.*

Work in patt from Chart B.
Row 1 Work one st before patt rep,
[work across 6-st patt rep] 3 times, then
work one st after patt.
Row 2 Work one st before patt rep,
[work across 6-st patt rep] 3 times, then
work one st after patt.
These 2 rows set the Chart.
Cont in patt to end of row 16, then rep
rows 1 to 16 until piece measures approx
12in/30cm from colored threads, ending on
a p row in A.
Leave these sts on a holder.

HANDLES (make 2)
Using size 5 (3.75mm) needles and A,
cast on 21 sts.
Next row K5, sl 1pw, k9, sl 1pw, k5.

KEY
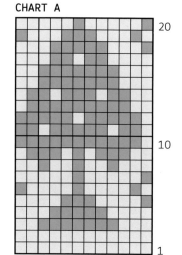
☐ Clay 177 (A)
■ Gilt 160 (B)
■ Celadon 184 (C)
■ Damask 182 (D)
■ Maritime 167 (E)

Next row P to end.
Rep the last 2 rows 64 times more.
Bind off.

LINING
BACK AND FRONT (both alike)
Using size 3 (3.25mm) needles and A,
cast on 74 sts.
Beg with a k row, cont in St st and
stripes as folls:
[2 rows A, 2 rows C] 5 times, then [1 row
A, 3 rows B, 1 row A, 3 rows D, 1 row A,
3 rows E, 1 row A, 3 rows C] until work
measures same as main piece.
Leave these sts on a holder.

GUSSET (make 2)
Using size 3 (3.25mm) needles and A,
cast on 18 sts.
Beg with a k row, work in St st until
piece fits from halfway across cast-on
edge, ending with a p row.
Beg with a k row, work in St st and
stripes as folls:
[2 rows A, 2 rows C] 5 times, then [1 row
A, 3 rows B, 1 row A, 3 rows D, 1 row A,
3 rows E, 1 row A, 3 rows C] until same

CHART A

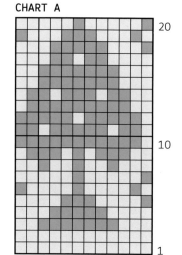

12-st patt rep

CHART B

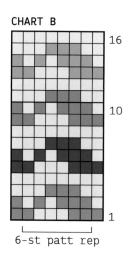

6-st patt rep

CHART C

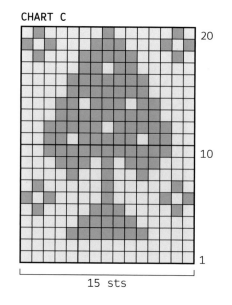

15 sts

number of "stripes" have been worked as on main piece.
Leave these sts on a holder.

FINISHING

Join cast-on edges of gussets.

Sew row ends of gusset to row ends and cast-on edges of back and front. Make up lining in same way. With wrong sides together, place lining inside bag. Using size 3 (3.25mm) needles and A, k together one st from bag and one st from lining all round top edge.

Work in rounds.

Next round P to end.

Next round K to end.

Rep the last 2 rounds twice more.

Bind off purlwise.

Cut grosgrain ribbon in half. Place grosgrain ribbon along center of wrong side of handle and slip stitch in place along knitted slipped sts. Bring row ends of handle together, encasing grosgrain ribbon, and sew row ends together to form seam. Sew handles in place to inside of bag. For extra stiffness in bottom of bag, cut a piece of cardboard to fit along the base.

waves vest

FINISHED SIZE

To fit bust

32-34	36-38	40-42	in
81-86	91-97	102-107	cm

ACTUAL MEASUREMENTS

Bust

35½	39½	43½	in
90	100	110	cm

Length to shoulder

20	21	21½	in
51	53	55	cm

Longer length to shoulder

22	23	23½	in
56	58	60	cm

YARN

Rowan *Felted Tweed*
4(4:5) x 1¾oz/191yd balls in Camel 157 (A)
1 x 1¾oz/191yd ball in each of Ginger 154
(B) and Hedgerow 187 (C)

NEEDLES

Pair each of size 3 (3.25mm) and size 5
(3.75mm) knitting needles
Stitch holders

GAUGE

30 sts and 28 rows to 4in/10cm square
over patterned St st of Chart A using
size 5 (3.75mm) needles, or size to
obtain correct gauge.
23 sts and 32 rows to 4in/10cm square
over patterned St st of Chart B using
size 5 (3.75mm) needles, or size to
obtain correct gauge.

ABBREVIATIONS

See page 127.

NOTE

When working from chart, odd numbered rows
are knit rows and read from right to left.
Even numbered rows are purl rows and read
from left to right.
Use the Fair Isle method: strand the yarns
not in use across the wrong side of work,
weaving them under and over the working
yarn every 3 or 4 sts.

BACK

Using size 3 (3.25mm) needles and A,
cast on 103(115:127) sts.
Row 1 K1, [p1, k1] to end.
Row 2 P1, [k1, p1] to end.
Rep the last 2 rows 13 times more and
row 1 again.
Inc row Rib 5(11:17), m1, [rib 3, m1]
31 times, rib 5(11:17).
135(147:159) sts.
Change to size 5 (3.75mm) needles.
Cont in patt from Chart A.
Row 1 Work 2 sts before patt rep, [work
across 12-st patt rep] 11(12:13) times,
work one st after patt rep.
Row 2 Work one st before patt rep, [work
across 12-st patt rep] 11(12:13) times,
work 2 sts after patt rep.
These 2 rows set the Chart A.
Cont to work in patt from Chart A to end
of row 29.
Dec row P4(10:16), p2tog, [p2, p2tog]
31 times, p5(11:17). *103(115:127) sts.*
Cont in patt from Chart B.
Row 1 Work 4 sts before patt rep, [work
across 12-st patt rep] 8(9:10) times, work
3 sts after patt rep.
Row 2 Work 3 sts before patt rep, [work
across 12-st patt rep] 8(9:10) times, work
4 sts after patt rep.
These 2 rows set Chart B.
Work in patt to end of row 6.
These 6 rows set the patt.
Work even until back measures 12(12½:13)in/

31(32:33)cm from cast-on edge, ending with a p row.

For longer length work 14(14½:15)in/ 36(37:38)cm from cast-on edge, ending with a p row.

SHAPE ARMHOLES

Keeping patt correct:

Bind off 9(10:11) sts at beg of next 2 rows.

85(95:105) sts.

Next row K1, skpo, patt to last 3 sts, k2tog, k1.

Next row P1, p2tog, patt to last 3 sts, p2tog tbl, p1.

Rep the last 2 rows once more.

77(87:97) sts.

Next row K1, skpo, patt to last 3 sts, k2tog, k1.

Next row Patt to end.

Rep the last 2 rows 3(5:7) times more.

69(75:81) sts.

Next row K1, skpo, patt to last 3 sts, k2tog, k1.

Work 3 rows.

Next row K1, skpo, patt to last 3 sts, k2tog, k1. *65(71:77) sts.*

Work even until back measures 19½(20:21) in/49(51:53)cm from cast-on edge, ending with a p row.

For longer length work even until back measures 21½(22:23)in/54(56:58)cm from cast-on edge, ending with a p row.

SHAPE SHOULDERS AND BACK NECK

Bind off 5(6:7) sts at beg of next 2 rows.

Next row Bind off 5(6:7) sts, patt until there are 10 sts on the needle, turn and work on these sts for first side of neck.

Next row Bind off 4 sts, patt to end.

Bind off rem 6 sts.

With right side facing, slip center 25(27:29) sts on a holder, rejoin yarn to rem sts, patt to end.

Next row Bind off 5(6:7) sts, patt to end.

Next row Bind off 4 sts, patt to end.

Bind off rem 6 sts.

CHART A

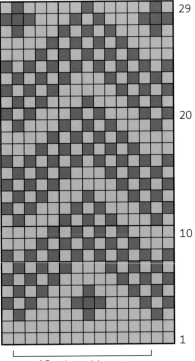

29

20

10

1

12-st patt rep

CHART B

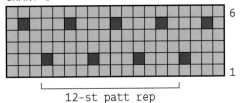

6

1

12-st patt rep

KEY

☐ Camel 157 (A)

■ Ginger 154 (B)

■ Hedgerow 187 (C)

FRONT

Work as given for Back until front is 8 rows less than back to armhole shaping, ending with a p row.

SHAPE FRONT NECK

Keeping patt correct:

Next row Patt 48(54:60), k2tog, k1, turn and work on these sts.

Work 3 rows.

Next row Patt to last 3 sts, k2tog, k1.

Work 3 rows.

SHAPE ARMHOLE

Next row Bind off 9(10:11) sts, patt to last 3 sts, k2tog, k1. *39(44:49) sts.*

Next row Patt to end.

Next row K1, skpo, patt to end.

Next row Patt to last 3 sts, p2tog tbl, p1.

Next row K1, skpo, patt to last 3 sts, k2tog, k1.

Next row Patt to last 3 sts, p2tog tbl, p1. *34(39:44) sts.*

Next row K1, skpo, patt to end.

Next row Patt to end.

Next row K1, skpo, patt to last 3 sts, k2tog, k1.

Next row Patt to end.

Rep the last 4 rows 1(2:3) time(s) more. *28(30:32) sts.*

Next row K1, skpo, patt to end.

Next row Patt to end.

Next row Patt to last 3 sts, k2tog, k1.

Next row Patt to end.

Next row K1, skpo, patt to end. *25(27:29) sts.*

Keeping armhole edge straight, cont to dec at neck edge on every 2nd and 4th row until 16(18:20) sts rem.

Work even until front measures the same as back to shoulder shaping, ending at armhole edge.

SHAPE SHOULDER

Next row Bind off 5(6:7) sts at beg of next and foll right side row.

Work 1 row.

Bind off rem 6 sts.

With right side facing, place center st on a safety pin, rejoin yarn to rem sts, k1, skpo, patt to end.

Work 3 rows.

Next row K1, skpo, patt to end.

Rep the last 4 rows once more.

SHAPE ARMHOLE

Next row Bind off 9(10:11) sts, patt to end. *39(44:49) sts.*

Next row Patt to last 3 sts, k2tog, k1.

Next row P1, p2tog, patt to end.

Next row K1, skpo, patt to last 3 sts, k2tog, k1.

Next row P1, p2tog, patt to end. *34(39:44) sts.*

Next row Patt to last 3 sts, k2tog, k1.

Next row Patt to end.

Next row K1, skpo, patt to last 3 sts, k2tog, k1.

Next row Patt to end.

Rep the last 4 rows 1(2:3) time(s) more. *28(30:32) sts.*

Next row Patt to last 3 sts, k2tog, k1.

Next row Patt to end.

Next row K1, skpo, patt to end.

Next row Patt to end.

Next row Patt to last 3 sts, k2tog, k1. *25(27:29) sts.*

Keeping armhole edge straight, cont to dec at neck edge on every 2nd and 4th row until 16(18:20) sts rem.

Work even until front measures the same as back to shoulder shaping, ending at armhole edge.

SHAPE SHOULDER

Next row Bind off 5(6:7) sts at beg of next and foll wrong side row.

Work 1 row.

Bind off rem 6 sts.

NECKBAND

Join right shoulder seam.

With right side facing, using size 3 (3.25mm) needles and A, pick up and k56(58:60) sts down left side of front neck, k1 st from safety pin, pick up and k56(58:60) sts up right side of front neck, 8 sts down right side of back neck,

k across 25(27:29) sts
from back neck holder,
pick up and k7 sts up
left side of back neck.
153(159:165) sts.
Next row P1, [k1, p1] to
end.
This row sets the rib.
Next row Rib 54(56:58),
k2tog, k1, skpo, rib to
end.
Rib 1 row.
Next row Rib 53(55:57),
k2tog, k1, skpo, rib to
end.
Rib 1 row.
Next row Rib 52(54:56),
k2tog, k1, skpo, rib to
end.
Rib 1 row.
Bind off in rib,
decreasing on this row
as before.

ARMBANDS (both alike)

Join shoulder seams. Join
left shoulder and neckband
seam.
With right side facing,
using size 3 (3.25mm)
needles and A, pick up and
k123(129:135) sts evenly
round armhole edge.
Work 7 rows rib as given
for Back.
Bind off in rib.

FINISHING

Join side and armband
seams.

little hearts vest

FINISHED SIZE
To fit bust

32-34	36-38	40-42	in
81-86	91-97	102-107	cm

ACTUAL MEASUREMENTS
Bust

37	41	45	in
94	104	114	cm

Length to back neck

20	20¾	21½	in
51	53	55	cm

YARN
Rowan *Felted Tweed*
3(4:4) x 1¾oz/191yd balls in Clay 177 (A)
1 x 1¾oz/191yd ball in each of Tawny 186
(B), Avocado 161 (C), Cinnamon 175 (D),
Peony 183 (E), Duck Egg 173 (F), and
Watery 152 (G)

NEEDLES
Pair each of size 3 (3.25mm) and size 5
(3.75mm) knitting needles

GAUGE
24 sts and 28 rows to 4in/10cm square
over patterned St st using size 5
(3.75mm) needles.
23 sts and 32 rows to 4in/10cm square
over St st using size 5 (3.75mm) needles,
or size to obtain correct gauge.

ABBREVIATIONS
See page 127.

NOTE
When working from chart, odd numbered
rows are knit rows and read from right
to left. Even numbered rows are purl rows
and read from left to right.
Use the Fair Isle method: strand the
yarns not in use across the wrong side
of work, weaving them under and over the
working yarn every 3 or 4 sts.

BACK
Using size 3 (3.25mm) needles and A,
cast on 111(123:135) sts.
Row 1 K1, [p1, k1] to end.
Row 2 P1, [k1, p1] to end.
Rep the last 2 rows 9 times more.
Change to size 5 (3.75mm) needles.
Cont in patt from Chart.
Row 1 Work 2 sts before patt rep, [work
across row 1 of 12-st patt rep] 9(10:11)
times, work one st after patt rep.
Row 2 Work one st before patt rep, [work
across row 2 of 12-st patt rep] 9(10:11)
times, work 2 sts after patt rep.
These 2 rows set the chart.
Cont to work in patt from Chart to end of
row 42.
Cont in St st and stripes of 2 rows B,
2 rows A, 2 rows C, 2 rows A, 2 rows D,
2 rows A, 2 rows E, 2 rows A, 2 rows F,
2 rows A, 2 rows G, 2 rows A, until back
measures 12¼(12½:13)in/31(32:33)cm from
cast-on edge, ending with a p row **.
SHAPE ARMHOLES
Bind off 10(11:12) sts at beg of next 2
rows. *91(101:111) sts.*
Next row K1, skpo, k to last 3 sts,
k2 tog, k1.
Next row P1, p2tog, p to last 3 sts,
p2 tog tbl, p1.
Rep the last 2 rows twice more.
79(89:99) sts.
Next row K1, skpo, k to last 3 sts,
k2tog, k1.
Next row P to end.
Rep the last 2 rows 6(8:10) times more.
65(71:77) sts.
Work even until back measures
19½(20½:21½)in/50(52:54)cm from cast-on
edge, ending with a p row.
SHAPE SHOULDERS AND BACK NECK
Bind off 5(6:7) sts at beg of next 2
rows. *55(59:63) sts.*
Next row Bind off 5(6:7) sts, k until

there are 10 sts on the needle, turn and
work on these sts for first side of neck.
Next row Bind off 4 sts, patt to end.
Bind off rem 6 sts.
With right side facing, slip center
25(27:29) sts onto a holder, rejoin yarn
to rem sts, patt to end.
Next row Bind off 5(6:7) sts, p to end.
Next row Bind off 4 sts, k to end.
Bind off rem 6 sts.

FRONT

Work as given for Back to **.
SHAPE ARMHOLE AND FRONT NECK
Next row K1, skpo, k32(36:40), k2tog, k1,
turn and work on these sts for first side
of neck. *36(40:44) sts.*
Next row P to last 3 sts, p2tog tbl, p1.
Next row K1, skpo, k to last 3 sts,
k2tog, k1.
Next row P to last 3 sts, p2tog tbl, p1.
Rep the last 2 rows once more.
29(33:37) sts.
Next row K1, skpo, k to last 3 sts,
k2tog, k1.
Next row P to end.
Next row K1, skpo, k to end.
Next row P to end.
Rep the last 4 rows 2(3:4) times and the
first 2 rows again. *18(19:20) sts.*
For 1st and 2nd sizes only
Keeping armhole edge straight, cont to
dec at neck edge on 3rd and foll 4th(0)
row until 16(18) sts rem.
For all sizes
Work even until front measures the same
as back to shoulder shaping, ending at
armhole edge.
SHAPE SHOULDER
Bind off 5(6:7) sts at beg of next and
foll right side row.
Work 1 row.
Bind off rem 6 sts.
With right side facing, slip center
15(17:19) sts onto a holder, rejoin yarn
to rem sts, k1, skpo, k to last 3 sts,
k2tog, k1. *36(40:44) sts.*

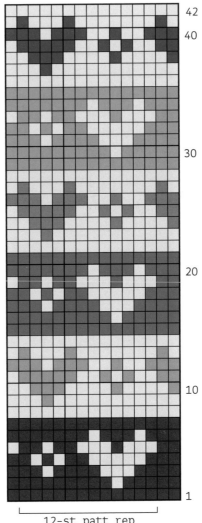

12-st patt rep

KEY
- ☐ Clay 177 (A)
- ■ Tawny 186 (B)
- ■ Avocado 161 (C)
- ■ Cinnamon 175 (D)
- ■ Peony 183 (E)
- ■ Duck Egg 173 (F)
- ■ Watery 152 (G)

Next row P1, p2tog, p to end.
Next row K1, skpo, k to last 3 sts, k2tog, k1.
Next row P1, p2tog, p to end.
Rep the last 2 rows once more.
29(33:37) sts.
Next row K1, skpo, k to last 3 sts, k2tog, k1.
Next row P to end.
Next row K to last 3 sts, k2tog, k1.
Next row P to end.
Rep the last 4 rows 2(3:4) times and the first 2 rows again.
18(19:20) sts.

For 1st and 2nd sizes only
Keeping armhole edge straight, cont to dec at neck edge on 3rd and foll 4th(0) row until 16(18) sts rem.

For all sizes
Work even until front measures the same as back to shoulder shaping, ending at armhole edge.

SHAPE SHOULDER
Bind off 5(6:7) sts at beg of next and foll wrong side row.
Work 1 row.
Bind off rem 6 sts.

NECKBAND
Join right shoulder seam.
With right side facing, using size 3 (3.25mm) needles and A, pick up and k48(51:54) sts down left side of front neck, k15(17:19) sts from front neck holder, pick up and k48(51:54) sts up right side of front neck, 6 sts down right side of back neck, k25(27:29) sts from back neck holder, pick up and k6 sts up left side of back neck. *148(158:168) sts.*
Rib row [K1, p1] to end.
Rep this row 4 times more.
Bind off in rib.

ARMBANDS
Join shoulder seams.
With right side facing, using size 3 (3.25mm) needles and A, pick up and k108(116:122) sts evenly round armhole edge.
Rib row [K1, p1] to end.
Rep this row 4 times more.
Bind off in rib.

FINISHING
Join side and armband seams.

folk warmer

FINISHED SIZE
47in/120cm all round by 14in/35cm deep

YARN
Rowan *Felted Tweed*
3 x 1¾oz/191yd balls in Granite 191 (A)
1 x 1¾oz/191yd ball in Clay 177 (B)
Small amounts of Avocado 161, Peony 183,
and Watery 152 for embroidery

NEEDLES
Pair each of size 3 (3.25mm) and 3.75mm
(US 5) knitting needles

GAUGE
24 sts and 28 rows to 4in/10cm square over
patterned St st using size 5 (3.75mm)
needles, or size to obtain correct gauge.

ABBREVIATIONS
See page 127.

NOTE
When working from chart, right side rows
are knit rows and read from right to left.
Wrong side rows are purl rows and read
from left to right.
Use the Fair Isle method: strand the yarns
not in use across the wrong side of work,
weaving them under and over the working
yarn every 3 or 4 sts.

BACK
Using size 3 (3.25mm) needles and A,
cast on 146 sts.
Rib row 1 K2, [p2, k2] to end.
Rib row 2 P2, [k2, p2] to end.
These 2 rows form the rib.
Work a further 8 rows.
Change to size 5 (3.75mm) needles.
Join in B.
Beg with a k row, work in St st.
Work 1 row B, 1 row A, 1 row B, 2 rows A.
Cont in patt from Chart A.

Row 1 P1A, [work across 12-st patt rep]
12 times, p1A.
Row 2 K1A, [work across 12-st patt rep]
12 times, k1A.
These 2 rows set the chart.
Cont to work in patt from chart to end of
row 5.
Work 2 rows A, 1 row B, 1 row A, 1 row B,
2 rows A.
Cont in patt from Chart B.
Row 1 P1A, [work across 24-st patt rep]
6 times, p1A.
Row 2 K1A, [work across 24-st patt rep]
6 times, k1A.
These 2 rows set the chart.
Cont to work in patt from chart to end of
row 13.
SHAPE SIDES
Work 2 rows A, 1 row B, 1 row A, 1 row B,
at the same time dec one st at each end
of every right side row. *140 sts.*
Cont in patt from Chart C.
Row 1 Using A, p to end.
Row 2 Using A, Skpo, work 8 sts before
patt rep, [work across 8-st patt rep]
15 times, work 8 sts after patt rep,
using A k2tog. *138 sts.*
Row 3 P1A, work 8 sts before patt rep,
[work across 8-st patt rep] 15 times,
work 8 sts after patt rep, p1B.
These 2 rows **set** the chart.
Cont to work in patt from chart, dec one
st at each end of every right side row to
end of row 15. *126 sts.*
Now work in main spot patt as set by rows
10 to 15 of Chart C.**
Dec one st at each end of next 11 right
side rows. *104 sts.*
Now dec one st at each end of next 11
rows. *82 sts.*
SHAPE SHOULDERS
Bind off 6 sts at beg of next 6 rows.
46 sts.
Leave these sts on a spare needle.

CHART A

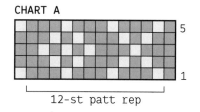

5

1

12-st patt rep

CHART B

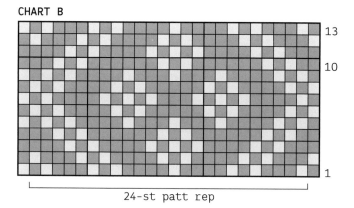

13

10

1

24-st patt rep

CHART C

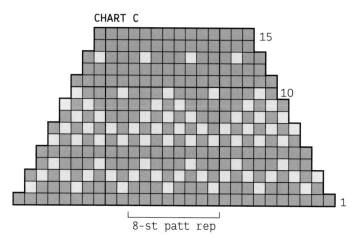

15

10

1

8-st patt rep

KEY

■ Granite 191 (A)
□ Clay 177 (B)

FRONT

Work as given for Back to **.

SHAPE SIDES AND FRONT NECK

1st row Skpo, patt 48, turn and work on these sts for first side of neck.

2nd row P2tog, patt to end.

3rd row Skpo, patt to end.

Rep the last 2 rows 9 times more. *29 sts.*

22nd row Patt to last 2 sts, p2tog tbl.

23rd row Skpo, patt to end.

Rep the last 2 rows 4 times more and the first row again. *18 sts.*

SHAPE SHOULDER

Bind off 6 sts at beg of next and foll right side row. *6 sts.*

Work 1 row.

Bind off rem 6 sts.

With right side facing, slip center 26 sts onto a holder, rejoin yarn to rem sts, patt to last 2 sts, k2tog. *49 sts.*

2nd row Patt to last 2 sts, p2tog tbl.

3rd row Patt to last 2 sts, k2tog.

Rep the last 2 rows 9 times more. *29 sts.*

22nd row P2tog, patt to end.

23rd row Patt to last 2 sts, k2tog.

Rep the last 2 rows 4 times more and the first row again. *18 sts.*

Work 1 row.

SHAPE SHOULDER

Bind off 6 sts at beg of next and foll

wrong side row. *6 sts.*
Work 1 row.
Bind off rem 6 sts.

COLLAR

Join right shoulder and side seam.
With right side facing, using size 3
(3.25mm) needles and A, pick up and k36
sts down left side of front neck, k
across 26 sts from front neck holder,
pick up and k35 sts up right side of
front neck, k46 sts from back neck
holder. *143 sts.*
Rib row 1 P2, [k1, p2] to end.

Rib row 2 K2, [p1, k2] to end.
These 2 rows form the rib.
Work a further 22 rows.
Inc row P2, [k1, m1, p2] to end. *190 sts.*
Next row K2, [p2, k2] to end.
Change to size 5 (3.75mm) needles.
Cont in rib as set until collar measures
7in/18cm, ending with a wrong side row.
Bind off in rib.

FINISHING

Join left shoulder, side, and collar
seam. Using chain st, lazy daisy st, and
French knots, embroider as illustrated.

folk cowl

FINISHED SIZE
31½in/80cm all round by 10¾in/27cm deep

YARN
Rowan *Felted Tweed*
2 x 1¾oz/191yd balls in Granite 191 (A)
1 x 1¾oz/191yd ball in Clay 177 (B)
Small amounts of Avocado 161, Peony 183, and Watery 152 for embroidery

NEEDLES
Pair each of size 3 (3.25mm) and size 5 (3.75mm) knitting needles

GAUGE
24 sts and 28 rows to 4in/10cm square over patterned St st using size 5 (3.75mm) needles, or size to obtain correct gauge.

ABBREVIATIONS
See page 127.

NOTE
When working from chart, right side rows are knit rows and read from right to left. Wrong side rows are purl rows and read from left to right.
Use the Fair Isle method: strand the yarns not in use across the wrong side of work, weaving them under and over the working yarn every 3 or 4 sts.

BACK AND FRONT (both alike)
Using size 3 (3.25mm) needles and A, cast on 98 sts.
Rib row 1 K2, [p2, k2] to end.
Rib row 2 P2, [k2, p2] to end.
These 2 rows form the rib.
Work a further 8 rows.
Change to size 5 (3.75mm) needles.
Join in B.
Beg with a k row, work in St st.
Work 2 rows A, 1 row B, 1 row A, 1 row B, 2 rows A.
Cont in patt from Chart A.
Row 1 Work one st before patt rep, [work across 12-st patt rep] 8 times, work one st after patt rep.
Row 2 Work one st before patt rep, [work across 12-st patt rep] 8 times, work one st after patt rep.
These 2 rows set the chart.
Cont to work in patt from chart to end of row 5.
Work 2 rows A, 1 row B, 1 row A, 1 row B, 2 rows A.
Cont in patt from Chart B.
Row 1 Work one st before patt rep, [work across 24-st patt rep] 4 times, work one st after patt rep.
Row 2 Work one st before patt rep, [work across 24-st patt rep] 4 times, work one st after patt rep.
These 2 rows set the chart.
Cont to work in patt from Chart to end of row 13.
Work 2 rows A, 1 row B, 1 row A, 1 row B, 1 row A.
Cont in patt from Chart C.
Row 1 Work one st before patt rep, [work across 8-st patt rep] 12 times, work one st after patt rep.
Row 2 Work one st before patt rep, [work across 8-st patt rep] 12 times, work one st after patt rep.
These 2 rows set the chart.

CHART A

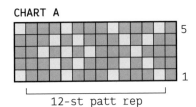

5

1

12-st patt rep

CHART C

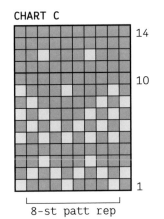

14

10

1

8-st patt rep

CHART B

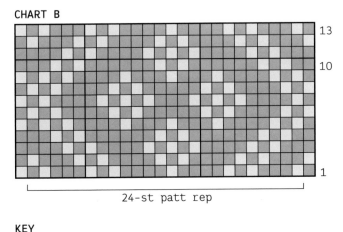

13

10

1

24-st patt rep

KEY

■ Granite 191 (A)
□ Clay 177 (B)

Cont to work in patt from chart to end of
row 14.
Now work in main spot patt as set by rows
9 to 14 of Chart C.
Work a further 9 rows.
Break off B.
Change to size 3 (3.25mm) needles.
Rib row 1 K2, [p2, k2] to end.
Rib row 2 P2, [k2, p2] to end.
These 2 rows form the rib.
Work a further 8 rows.
Bind off in rib.

FINISHING

Join side seams. Using chain st, lazy
daisy st, and French knots, embroider
as illustrated.

little owls cowl

FINISHED SIZE
9½in/24cm wide by 51in/130cm round

YARN
Rowan *Felted Tweed*
3 x 1¾oz/191yd balls in Clay 177 (A)
1 x 1¾oz/191yd ball in each of Cinnamon 175 (B), Ginger 154 (C), and Phantom 153 (D)

NEEDLES
Pair of size 5 (3.75mm) knitting needles
1 spare needle for bind off

GAUGE
23 sts and 32 rows to 4in/10cm square over patterned St st using 3.75mm (US 5) needles, or size to obtain correct gauge.

ABBREVIATIONS
See page 127.

NOTE
When working from chart, odd numbered rows are knit rows and read from right to left. Even numbered rows are purl rows and read from left to right.
Use the Fair Isle method: strand the yarns not in use across the wrong side of work, weaving them under and over the working yarn every 3 or 4 sts.

TO MAKE
FIRST SIDE
Using size 5 (3.75mm) needles and A, cast on 114 sts.
Beg with a k row, work in St st and patt from Chart A.
Row 1 Using A, k to end.
Row 2 [Work across row 2 of 14-st patt rep] 8 times, work 2 sts after patt rep.
Row 3 Work 2 sts before patt rep, [work across row 3 of 14-st patt rep] 8 times.
Rows 2 and 3 set Chart A.
Work in patt to end of row 50.
Work in patt from Chart B.
Dec row (this counts as row 1 of Chart)
Using A, k14, [k2tog, k26] 3 times, k2tog, k14. *110 sts.*
Row 2 [Work across row 2 of 12-st patt rep] 9 times, work 2 sts after patt rep.
Row 3 Work 2 sts before patt rep, [work across row 3 of 12-st patt rep] 9 times.
Rows 2 and 3 set Chart B.
Cont in patt until piece measures approx 25½in/65cm, ending with row 12.
Next row Using A, k to end.
Leave sts on a spare needle.
SECOND SIDE
With right side facing, using size 5 (3.75mm) needles and A, pick up and k110 sts along cast-on edge of first side.
Work in patt from Chart B.
Row 2 [Work across row 2 of 12-st patt rep] 9 times, work 2 sts after patt rep.
Row 3 Work 2 sts before patt rep, [work across row 3 of 12-st patt rep] 9 times.
Rows 2 and 3 set Chart B.
Cont in patt from Chart B until same number of rows have been worked as on first side, ending with row 12.
Work in patt from Chart A.
Inc row (this counts as row 1 of Chart)
Using A, k14, [m1, k27] 3 times, m1, k15. *114 sts.*

CHART A

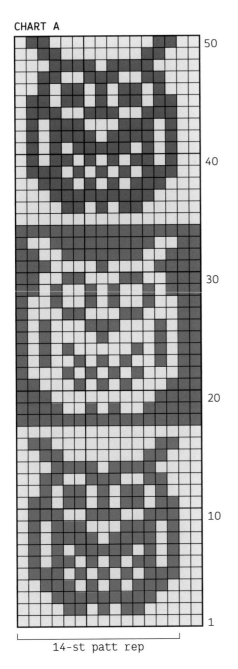

14-st patt rep

CHART B

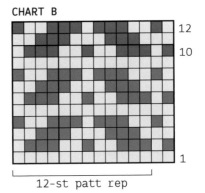

12-st patt rep

KEY

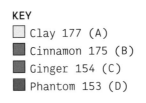

☐ Clay 177 (A)
◼ Cinnamon 175 (B)
◼ Ginger 154 (C)
◼ Phantom 153 (D)

Row 2 [Work across row 2 of 14-st patt rep] 8 times, work 2 sts after patt rep.
Row 3 Work 2 sts before patt rep, [work across row 3 of 14-st patt rep] 8 times.
Rows 2 and 3 set Chart A.
Work in patt to end of row 50.
Next row Using A, k to end, dec 4 sts evenly. *110 sts.*

FINISHING
With needles pointing in the same direction and right sides together, using A, bind off the sts of both pieces together.
Join row ends of cowl together.

little hearts cowl

FINISHED SIZE
31½in/80cm all round by 9½in/24cm deep

YARN
Rowan *Felted Tweed*
1 x 1¾oz/191yd ball in each of Clay 177 (A), Tawny 186 (B), Avocado 161 (C), Cinnamon 175 (D), Peony 183 (E), Duck Egg 173 (F), and Watery 152 (G)

NEEDLES
Pair each of size 3 (3.25mm) and size 5 (3.75mm) knitting needles

GAUGE
24 sts and 28 rows to 4in/10cm square over patterned St st using size 5 (3.75mm) needles, or size to obtain correct gauge.

ABBREVIATIONS
See page 127.

NOTE
When working from chart, odd numbered rows are knit rows and read from right to left. Even numbered rows are purl rows and read from left to right.
Use the Fair Isle method: strand the yarns not in use across the wrong side of work, weaving them under and over the working yarn every 3 or 4 sts.

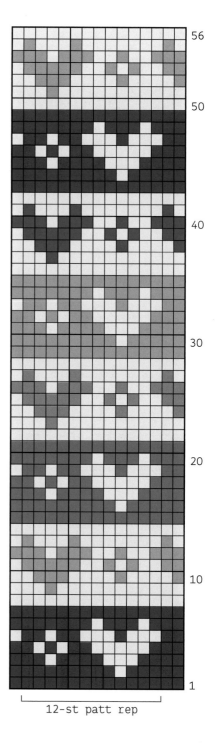

12-st patt rep

KEY

- ☐ Clay 177 (A)
- ■ Tawny 186 (B)
- ■ Avocado 161 (C)
- ■ Cinnamon 175 (D)
- ■ Peony 183 (E)
- ■ Duck Egg 173 (F)
- ■ Watery 152 (G)

BACK AND FRONT (both alike)
Using size 3 (3.25mm) needles and A,
cast on 98 sts.
Rib row [K1, p1] to end.
This row forms the rib.
Work a further 9 rows.
Change to size 5 (3.75mm) needles.
Cont in patt from Chart.
Row 1 Work one st before patt rep,
[work across row 1 of 12-st patt rep]
8 times, work one st after patt rep.
Row 2 Work one st before patt rep,
[work across row 2 of 12-st patt rep]
8 times, work one st after patt rep.
These 2 rows set the chart.
Cont to work in patt from Chart to end
of row 56.
Change to size 3 (3.25mm) needles.
Cont in A only.
Work 9 rows in rib.
Bind off in rib.

FINISHING
Join side seams.

plaid and diamond socks

FINISHED SIZE
To fit shoe size US 10-11/UK 9-10/EUR 43-44

YARN
Rowan *Felted Tweed*
2 x 1¾oz/191yd balls in Clay 177 (A)
1 x 1¾oz/191yd ball in each of Carbon 159
(B) and Cinnamon 175 (C)

NEEDLES
Set of 4 double-pointed size 5 (3.75mm)
knitting needles

GAUGE
23 sts and 32 rows to 4in/10cm square over
St st using size 5 (3.75mm) needles, or
size to obtain correct gauge.

ABBREVIATIONS
See page 127.

NOTE
When working from chart, all rows are knit
rows and read from right to left.
Use the Fair Isle method: strand the yarns
not in use across the wrong side of work,
weaving them under and over the working
yarn every 3 or 4 sts.

SOCKS (make 2)
Using size 5 (3.75mm) needles and A,
cast on 54 sts.
Arrange these sts on 3 needles and cont
in rounds.
Rib round [K1, p1] to end.
Rib a further 8 rounds.
Inc round Rib 2, m1, [rib 4, m1] to end.
68 sts.
Round 1 [Work 34-st patt rep 1st row of
Chart A on page 97] twice.
This round sets the Chart.
Cont in patt to end of round 21.
Round 22 K to end, dec 2 sts evenly.
66 sts.

Work in patt from Chart B on page 97.
Round 1 [Work 6 st patt rep] 11 times.
Work from Chart until round 10.
These 10 rounds set patt.
Cont in patt until work measures
12in/30cm from cast-on edge, ending with
a plain round.
Cont in A only.
Break off yarn.
Divide sts onto 3 needles as folls: slip
first 18 sts onto first needle, next 15 sts
onto second needle, and next 15 sts onto
3rd needle, slip last 18 sts onto other
end of first needle.

SHAPE HEEL
With right side facing, join yarn to 36
sts on first needle.
Work on these 36 sts only.
Working backward and forward in rows, not
rounds, work as folls:
Beg with a k row, work 20 rows St st.
Next row K26, skpo, turn.
Next row Sl 1, p16, p2tog, turn.
Next row Sl 1, k16, skpo, turn.
Next row Sl 1, p16, p2tog, turn.
Rep the last 2 rows 7 times more.
18 sts.
Break off yarn.
Reset sts on 3 needles as folls: slip
first 9 sts of heel sts onto a safety
pin, place marker here to indicate beg
of round. Join A to rem sts, with first
needle k9, then pick up and 14 sts along
side of heel, with second needle k30,
with 3rd needle pick up and k14 sts along
other side of heel, k9 from safety pin.
76 sts.
Cont in rounds.
K 1 round.
Dec round K23, k2tog, k26, k2tog tbl,
k23. *74 sts.*
K 1 round.
Dec round K22, k2tog, k26, k2tog tbl,
k22. *72 sts.*

K 1 round.
Dec round K21, k2tog, k26, k2tog tbl, k21. *70 sts.*
K 1 round.
Dec round K20, k2tog, k26, k2tog tbl, k20. *68 sts.*
K 1 round.
Dec round K19, k2tog, k26, k2tog tbl, k19. *66 sts.*
K 1 round.
Dec round K18, k2tog, k26, k2tog tbl, k18. *64 sts.*
K 1 round.
Cont in rounds of St st until sock measures 8¼in/21cm from back of heel.

SHAPE TOE
Next round K13, k2tog, k2, skpo, k26, k2tog, k2, skpo, k13. *60 sts.*
Next round K to end.
Next round K12, k2tog, k2, skpo, k24, k2tog, k2, skpo, k12. *56 sts.*
Next round K to end.
Next round K11, k2tog, k2, skpo, k22, k2tog, k2, skpo, k11. *52 sts.*
Next round K to end.
Cont in rounds decreasing on every alt round as set until the foll round has been worked.
Next round K5, k2tog, k2, skpo, k10, k2tog, k2, skpo, k5. *28 sts.*
Slip first 7 sts onto one needle, next 14 sts onto a second needle, then rem 7 sts on end of first needle.
Fold sock inside out and bind one st from each needle off together.

plaid and diamond beanie

FINISHED SIZE
To fit an average-sized man's head

YARN
Rowan *Felted Tweed*
1 x 1¾oz/191yd ball in each of Clay 177
(A), Carbon 159 (B), and Cinnamon 175 (C)

NEEDLES
Pair each of size 5 (3.75mm) and size 6
(4mm) knitting needles

GAUGE
22 sts and 30 rows to 4in/10cm over St st
using size 6 (4mm) needles, or size to
obtain correct gauge.

ABBREVIATIONS
See page 127.

NOTE
When working from chart, odd numbered
rows are knit rows and read from right
to left. Even numbered rows are purl rows
and read from left to right.
Use the Fair Isle method: strand the
yarns not in use across the wrong side
of work, weaving them under and over the
working yarn every 3 or 4 sts.

TO MAKE
Using size 5 (3.75mm) needles and A,
cast on 138 sts.
Rib row [K1, p1] to end.
Rep the last row 9 times more.
Change to size 6 (4mm) needles and work
in patt from Chart A.
Row 1 Work first st of patt rep, then
[work 34-st patt rep] 4 times, work one
st after patt rep.
Row 2 Work first st of patt rep, then
[work 34-st patt rep] 4 times, work one
st after patt rep.
These 2 rows set the patt.

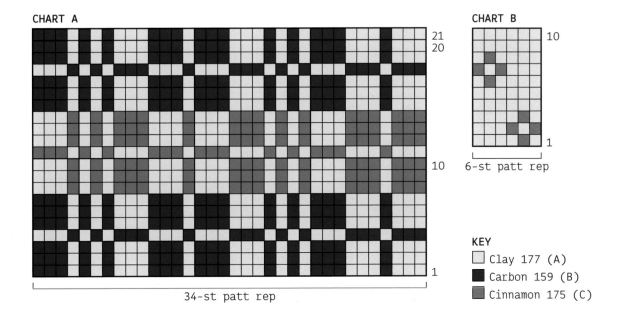

CHART A

21
20

10

1

34-st patt rep

CHART B

10

1

6-st patt rep

KEY
☐ Clay 177 (A)
■ Carbon 159 (B)
▨ Cinnamon 175 (C)

Cont in patt to end of row 21.
Row 22 Using A, p8, p2tog, [p6, p2tog]
15 times, p8. *122 sts.*
Work in patt from Chart B.
Row 1 Work first st of patt rep, then
[work 6-st patt rep] 20 times, work one
st after patt rep.
Row 2 Work first st of patt rep, then
[work 6-st patt rep] 20 times, work one
st after patt rep.
Work from Chart until row 10.
These 10 rows set the patt.
Cont in patt until hat measures
6¼in/16cm, ending after a wrong side row.
Cont in A only.
SHAPE CROWN
Row 1 K1, [skpo, k6] 15 times, k1.
107 sts.
Row 2 P to end.
Row 3 K1, [skpo, k5] 15 times, k1.
92 sts.
Row 4 P to end.
Row 5 K1, [skpo, k4] 15 times, k1.
77 sts.
Row 6 P to end.

Row 7 K1, [skpo, k3] 15 times, k1. *62 sts.*
Row 8 P to end.
Row 9 K1, [skpo, k2] 15 times, k1. *47 sts.*
Row 10 P to end.
Row 11 K1, [skpo, k1] 15 times, k1.
32 sts.
Row 12 P to end.
Row 13 K1, [skpo] 15 times, k1. *17 sts.*
Row 14 P to end.
Row 15 K2, [skpo] 7 times, k1. *10 sts.*
Leaving a long end, cut off yarn and
thread through rem sts.

FINISHING
Join back seam.

soft stripe gloves

FINISHED SIZE
To fit an average-sized woman's hand

YARN
Rowan *Felted Tweed*
2 x 1¾oz/191yd balls in Clay 177 (A)
1 x 1¾oz/191yd ball in each of Gilt 160
(B), Seasalter 178 (C), Duck Egg 173 (D),
and Celadon 184 (E)

NEEDLES
Pair each of size 3 (3.25mm) and size 5
(3.75mm) knitting needles

GAUGE
23 sts and 32 rows to 4in/10cm square
over St st using size 5 (3.75mm) needles,
or size to obtain correct gauge.

ABBREVIATIONS
See page 127.

NOTE
When working from chart, odd numbered
rows are knit rows and read from right
to left. Even numbered rows are purl rows
and read from left to right.
Use the Fair Isle method: strand the
yarns not in use across the wrong side
of work, weaving them under and over the
working yarn every 3 or 4 sts.

RIGHT GLOVE
** Using size 3 (3.25mm) needles and A,
cast on 52 sts.
Rib row [K1, p1] to end.
* Rep the last row twice more, dec one st
at center of last row. *51 sts.*
Change to size 5 (3.75mm) needles and
work in St st and patt from Chart.
Row 1 Work 2 sts before patt rep, then
[work 6-st patt rep] 8 times, work one st
after patt rep.
Row 2 Work one st before patt rep, then

[work 6-st patt rep] 8 times, work 2 sts
after patt rep.
These 2 rows set the patt.
Cont in patt to end of row 17, dec one st
at center of last row. *50 sts.*
Row 18 Using A, p to end.
Row 19 Using A, k to end.
Row 20 Using A, k to end to mark hemline.
Change to size 3 (3.25mm) needles.
Beg with a p row, cont in St st and
stripes of 2 rows A, then 3 rows E and 3
rows A.
Work a further 17 rows, ending with a p
row.
Change to size 5 (3.75mm) needles.
Work a further 12 rows **.
THUMB SHAPING
Next row K25, m1, k3, m1, k to end.
Work 3 rows.
Next row K25, m1, k5, m1, k to end.
Work 1 row.
Next row K25, m1, k7, m1, k to end.
Work 1 row.
Next row K25, m1, k9, m1, k to end.
Work 1 row. *58 sts.*
Cont to inc as set on every right side
row until there are 64 sts on needle.
Work 1 row.
Divide for thumb
Next row K42, turn.
Next row P17, turn.
Cont in A only.
Work 16 rows in St st.
Next row K1, [k2tog] to end. *9 sts.*
Break yarn, thread through rem sts, draw
up tightly, and join seam.
With right side facing, join yarn to base
of thumb, k to end. *47 sts.*
Work 15 rows.
Cont in A only.
*** Divide for fingers
FIRST FINGER
Next row K30, turn and cast on 2 sts.
Next row P15, turn.

Work 20 rows in St st.
Next row K1, [k2tog] to end. *8 sts.*
Break yarn, thread through rem sts, draw
up tightly, and join seam.

SECOND FINGER
With right side facing, join yarn to base
of first finger, pick up and k2 sts from
base of first finger, k6, turn, cast on 2
sts.
Next row P16, turn.
Work 24 rows in St st.
Next row [K2tog] to end. *8 sts.*
Break yarn, thread through rem sts, draw
up tightly, and join seam.

THIRD FINGER
With right side facing, join yarn to base
of second finger, pick up and k2 sts from
base of second finger, k6, turn, cast on
2 sts.
Next row P16, turn.
Work 20 rows in St st.
Next row [K2tog] to end. *8 sts.*
Break yarn, thread through rem sts, draw
up tightly, and join seam.

FOURTH FINGER
With right side facing, join yarn to base
of third finger, pick up and k2 sts from
base of third finger, k5, turn.
Next row P12.
Work 14 rows in St st.
Next row [K2tog] to end. *6 sts.*
Break yarn thread through rem sts, draw
up tightly, and join seam.

LEFT GLOVE
Work as given for Right Glove from **
to **.

THUMB SHAPING
Next row K22, m1, k3, m1, k to end.
Work 3 rows.
Next row K22, m1, k5, m1, k to end.
Work 1 row.
Next row K22, m1, k7, m1, k to end.
Work 1 row.
Next row K22, m1, k9, m1, k to end.
Work 1 row.
Cont to inc as set on every right side

row until there are 64 sts on needle.
Work 1 row.
Divide for thumb
Next row K39, turn.
Next row P17 sts, turn.
Cont in A only.
Work 16 rows in St st.
Next row K1, [k2tog] to end. *9 sts.*
Break yarn, thread through rem sts, draw
up tightly, and join seam.
With right side facing, join yarn in
correct color to base of thumb, k to end.
47 sts.
Work 15 rows.
Cont in A only.
Complete as for Right Glove from ***
to end.

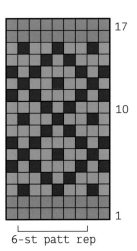

6-st patt rep

KEY
■ Gilt 160 (B)
■ Seasalter 178 (C)
■ Duck Egg 173 (D)

soft stripe beret

FINISHED SIZE
To fit an average-sized woman's head

YARN
Rowan *Felted Tweed*
1 x 1¾oz/191yd ball in each of Clay 177 (A), Gilt 160 (B) Seasalter 178 (C), Duck Egg 173 (D), and Celadon 184 (E)

NEEDLES
Pair each of size 5 (3.75mm) and size 6 (4mm) knitting needles

GAUGE
22 sts and 30 rows to 4in/10cm over patterned St st using size 6 (4mm) needles, or size to obtain correct gauge.

ABBREVIATIONS
See page 127.

TO MAKE
Using size 5 (3.75mm) needles and A, cast on 111 sts.
Rib row 1 K1, [p1, k1] to end.
Rib row 2 P1, [k1, p1] to end.
Rep the last 2 rows twice more and the first row again.
Inc row (WS) Rib 3, [m1, rib 3] to end.
147 sts.
Change to size 6 (4mm) needles and work in St st and patt from Chart on page 53.
Row 1 Work 2 sts before patt rep, then [work 6-st patt rep] 24 times, work one st after patt rep.
Row 2 Work first st before patt rep, then [work 6-st patt rep] 24 times, work 2 sts after patt rep.
These 2 rows set the patt.
Cont in patt to end of row 17.
Cont in St st and stripes of 3 rows A and 3 rows E as folls:
Row 18 Using A, p to end, dec one st at center of row.

146 sts.
Work 30 rows.

SHAPE CROWN
Row 1 K1, [skpo, k10] 12 times, k1.
134 sts.
Row 2 P to end.
Row 3 K1, [skpo, k9] 12 times, k1.
122 sts.
Row 4 P to end.
Row 5 K1, [skpo, k8] 12 times, k1.
110 sts.
Row 6 P to end.
Row 7 K1, [skpo, k7] 12 times, k1.
98 sts.
Row 8 P to end.
Row 9 K1, [skpo, k6] 12 times, k1.
86 sts.
Row 10 P to end.
Row 11 K1, [skpo, k5] 12 times, k1.
74 sts.
Row 12 P to end.
Row 13 K1, [skpo, k4] 12 times, k1.
62 sts.
Row 14 P to end.
Row 15 K1, [skpo, k3] 12 times, k1.
50 sts.
Row 16 P to end.
Row 17 K1, [skpo, k2] 12 times, k1.
38 sts.
Row 18 P to end.
Row 19 K1, [skpo, k1] 12 times, k1.
26 sts.
Row 20 P1, [p2tog] 12 times, p1.
14 sts.
Row 21 K1, [skpo] 6 times, k1.
8 sts.
Leaving a long end, cut off yarn and thread through rem sts.

FINISHING
Join seam.

little circles pillow

FINISHED SIZE
15in/38cm by 15in/38cm to fit a 16in/40cm square pillow form

YARN
Rowan *Felted Tweed*
3 x 1¾oz/191yd balls in Celadon 184 (A)
1 x 1¾oz/191yd ball in each of Tawny 186 (B) and Mineral 181 (C)

NEEDLES
Pair of size 5 (3.75mm) knitting needles

EXTRAS
16in/40cm pillow form

GAUGE
23 sts and 32 rows to 4in/10cm square over St st using size 5 (3.75mm) needles, or size to obtain correct gauge.

ABBREVIATIONS
See page 127.

NOTE
When working from chart, odd numbered rows are knit rows and read from right to left. Even numbered rows are purl rows and read from left to right.
Use the Fair Isle method: strand the yarns not in use across the wrong side of work, weaving them under and over the working yarn every 3 or 4 sts.

FRONT
Using size 5 (3.75mm) needles and A, cast on 92 sts.
Row 1 Using A, k to end.
Row 2 P2A, P[1C, 3A] to last 2 sts, 1C, 1A.
Row 3 Using A, k to end.
Row 4 Using A, p to end.
Row 5 K[3A, 1C] to end.
Row 6 Using A, p to end.

Rows 1 to 6 form the spot patt.
Work a further 43 rows, ending with row 1.
Work in St st and patt from Chart on page 34.
Row 50 Work one st before patt rep, [work across 5-st patt rep] 18 times, work one st after patt rep.
Row 51 Work one st before patt rep, [work across 5-st patt rep] 18 times, work one st after patt rep.
Rows 50 and 51 set the Chart.
Work in patt to end of row 12, then rows 3 to 7.
Rows 61 to 71 Rep rows 50 to 60 once, and row 50 again.
Rows 72 to 120 Rep rows 1 to 6 eight times and row 1 again.
Using A, bind off.

BACK
Using size 5 (3.75mm) needles and A, cast on 92 sts.
Row 1 Using A, k to end.
Row 2 P2A, P[1C, 3A] to last 2 sts, 1C, 1A.
Row 3 Using A, k to end.
Row 4 Using A, p to end.
Row 5 K[3A, 1C] to end.
Row 6 Using A, p to end.
Rows 1 to 6 form the spot patt.
Rows 7 to 120 Rep rows 1 to 6 nineteen times more.
Using A, bind off.

FINISHING
With right sides together, sew back to front along three sides. Insert pillow form, join rem side.

simple spots pillow

FINISHED SIZE
15in/38cm by 15in/38cm to fit a 16in/40cm square pillow form

YARN
Rowan *Felted Tweed*
1 x 1¾oz/191yd ball in each of Frozen 185 (A), Cinnamon 175 (B), Avocado 161 (C), Tawny 186 (D), and Maritime 167 (E)

NEEDLES
Pair of size 5 (3.75mm) knitting needles

EXTRAS
16in/40cm pillow form

GAUGE
23 sts and 32 rows to 4in/10cm square over St st using size 5 (3.75mm) needles. 24 sts and 32 rows to 4in/10cm square over patt using size 5 (3.75mm) needles, or size to obtain correct gauge.

ABBREVIATIONS
See page 127.

NOTE
When working from chart, odd numbered rows are knit rows and read from right to left. Even numbered rows are purl rows and read from left to right.
Use the Fair Isle method: strand the yarns not in use across the wrong side of work, weaving them under and over the working yarn every 3 or 4 sts.

FRONT
Using size 5 (3.75mm) needles and A, cast on 91 sts.
P 1 row.
Work in patt.
Row 1 Work 3 sts before patt rep, [work across 8-st patt rep] 11 times.
Row 2 [Work across 8-st patt rep] 11

times, work 3 sts after patt rep.
These 2 rows set the Chart.
Work in patt to end of row 20.
These 20 rows set the patt.
Work a further 100 rows.
Row 121 Using A, k to end.
Bind off.

BACK
Using size 5 (3.75mm) needles and A, cast on 87 sts.
P 1 row.
Beg with a k row, work in St st and stripes of [5 rows B, 5 rows E, 5 rows D, 5 rows C] 6 times, see photograph on page 105, right.
Row 121 Using A, k to end.
Bind off.

FINISHING
With right sides together, sew back to front along three sides. Insert pillow form, join rem side.

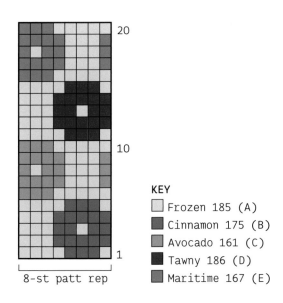

KEY
☐ Frozen 185 (A)
■ Cinnamon 175 (B)
■ Avocado 161 (C)
■ Tawny 186 (D)
■ Maritime 167 (E)

8-st patt rep

paper dolls pillow

FINISHED SIZE
15in/38cm by 15in/38cm to fit a 16in/40cm square pillow form

YARN
Rowan *Felted Tweed*
2 x 1¾oz/191yd balls in Duck Egg 173 (A)
1 x 1¾oz/191yd ball in each of Tawny 186 (B), Mineral 181 (C), and Hedgerow 187 (D)

NEEDLES
Pair of size 5 (3.75mm) knitting needles

EXTRAS
16in/40cm pillow form

GAUGE
23 sts and 32 rows to 4in/10cm square over St st using size 5 (3.75mm) needles. 24 sts and 32 rows to 4in/10cm square over patt St St using size 5 (3.75mm) needles, or size to obtain correct gauge.

ABBREVIATIONS
See page 127.

NOTE
When working from chart, odd numbered rows are knit rows and read from right to left. Even numbered rows are purl rows and read from left to right.
Use the Fair Isle method: strand the yarns not in use across the wrong side of work, weaving them under and over the working yarn every 3 or 4 sts.

FRONT
Using size 5 (3.75mm) needles and A, cast on 91 sts.
P 1 row.
Work in patt from Chart A.
Row 1 (RS) Work 2 sts before patt rep, then [work across 8-st patt rep] 11 times, work one st after patt rep.

Row 2 Work one st before patt rep, [work across 8-st patt rep] 11 times, work 2 sts after patt rep.
These 2 rows set Chart A.
Work in patt to end of row 23.
Work in patt from Chart B.
Row 1 (WS) [Work across 7-st patt rep] 13 times.
Row 2 [Work across 7-st patt rep] 13 times.
These 2 rows set Chart B.
Work in patt to end of row 9.
These 32 rows set the patt.
Work a further 87 rows, ending row 23 of Chart A.
Bind off.

BACK
Using size 5 (3.75mm) needles and A, cast on 87 sts.
P 1 row.
Beg with a k row, work in St st and stripes of:
1 row A, 3 rows C, [3 rows A, 1 row B] 3 times, 3 rows A = 15 rows.
3 rows C **, [1 row A, 2 rows D] 3 times, 1 row A = 10 rows.
These 32 rows form the stripe sequence; see photograph on page 105, left.
Work a further 86 rows, ending row at **.
Work 1 row A.
Bind off.

FINISHING
With right sides together, sew back to front along three sides. Insert pillow form, join rem side.

CHART A

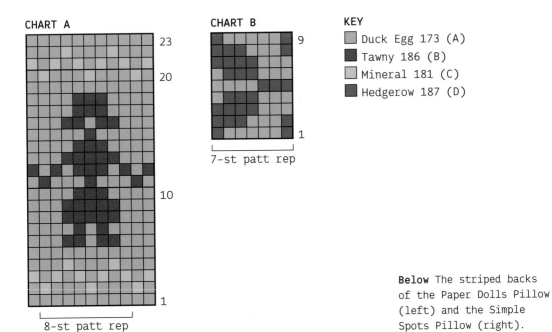

23

20

10

1

8-st patt rep

CHART B

9

1

7-st patt rep

KEY
- ⬜ Duck Egg 173 (A)
- ⬛ Tawny 186 (B)
- ⬜ Mineral 181 (C)
- 🟩 Hedgerow 187 (D)

Below The striped backs of the Paper Dolls Pillow (left) and the Simple Spots Pillow (right).

nordic pillow

FINISHED SIZE
11in/28cm by 11in/28cm to fit a 12in/30cm square pillow form

YARN
Rowan *Felted Tweed*
One x 1¾oz/191yd ball in each of Avocado 161 (A) and Rage 150 (B)
Approx ½oz of Mineral 181 (C)
Small amount of Phantom 153 (D) and Seasalter 178 (E)
You will need approx 5oz of assorted colors altogether

NEEDLES
Pair each of size 2 (2.75mm) and size 5 (3.75mm) knitting needles

EXTRAS
12in/30cm pillow form

GAUGE
23 sts and 32 rows to 4in/10cm square over St st using size 5 (3.75mm) needles, or size to obtain correct gauge.

ABBREVIATIONS
See page 127.

NOTE
When working from chart, odd numbered rows are knit rows and read from right to left. Even numbered rows are purl rows and read from left to right.
Use the Fair Isle method: strand the yarns not in use across the wrong side of work, weaving them under and over the working yarn every 3 or 4 sts.

PLAIN SQUARE (make 2)
Leaving a long end of approx 12in/30cm, using size 5 (3.75mm) needles and A, cast on 37 sts.
Beg with a k row, work 44 rows in St st.

Leaving a long end of approx 12in/30cm, bind off.

BIRD'S EYE SQUARE (make 2)
Leaving a long end of approx 12in/30cm, using size 5 (3.75mm) needles and B, cast on 37 sts.
Row 1 Using B, k to end.
Row 2 P to end.
Row 3 K4B, [1C, 3B] to last 5 sts, 1C, 4B.
Row 4 Using B, p to end.
Row 5 K to end.
Row 6 P2M, [1C, 3M] to last 3 sts, 1C, 2M.
These 6 rows form the patt.
Work a further 38 rows, ending row 2.
Leaving a long end of approx 12in/30cm, bind off.

GARTER ST NORDIC TREE
(make 2)
TRUNK
Leaving a long end of approx 8in/20cm, using size 2 (2.75mm) needles and D, cast on 5 sts.
K 10 rows.
Leave these sts on a spare needle.
MAIN PART
Leaving a long end of approx 12in/30cm, using size 2 (2.75mm) needles and E, cast on 15 sts.
Row 1 (RS) K5, with right side of trunk to wrong side of cast-on row, [k1tog with one st from trunk] 5 times, k5.
Row 2 K to end.
Row 3 Skpo, k to last 2 sts, k2tog. *13 sts.*
K 3 rows.
Rep the last 4 rows 5 times more. *3 sts.*
K3tog and leaving a long end, fasten off.

FAIR ISLE NORDIC TREE
(make 2)

TRUNK
Leaving a long end of approx 8in/20cm, using size 2 (2.75mm) needles and D, cast on 7 sts.
K 10 rows.
Leave these sts on a spare needle.

MAIN PART
Leaving a long end of approx 12in/30cm, using size 2 (2.75mm) needles and B, cast on 27 sts.

Row 1 K10, with right side of trunk to wrong side of cast-on row, [k1tog with one st from trunk] 7 times, k10.
Row 2 P to end.
Work in patt from row 3 of Chart, shaping as shown.

BACK
Using size 5 (3.75mm) needles and color of choice (we used B), cast on 71 sts.
Work 88 rows in 4 row stripes in colors of choice.
Bind off.

FINISHING
Sew trees to squares. Join squares to form the front.
With right sides together, sew back to front along 3 sides. Insert pillow form, join rem side.

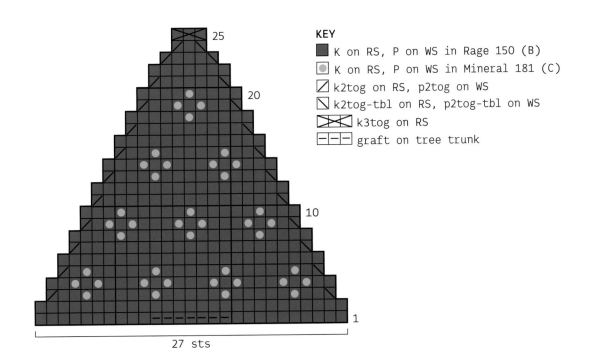

KEY
- ■ K on RS, P on WS in Rage 150 (B)
- ⦿ K on RS, P on WS in Mineral 181 (C)
- ╱ k2tog on RS, p2tog on WS
- ╲ k2tog-tbl on RS, p2tog-tbl on WS
- ⊠ k3tog on RS
- ⊟ graft on tree trunk

27 sts

goosey pillow

FINISHED SIZE
19in/48cm by 11in/28cm to fit a 20in/50cm
by 12in/30cm pillow form

YARN
Rowan *Felted Tweed*
2 x 1¾oz/191yd balls in each of Clay 177
(A) and Avocado 161 (B)
1 x 1¾oz/191yd ball in Seasalter 178 (C)

NEEDLES
Pair of size 5 (3.75mm) knitting needles

EXTRAS
20in/50cm by 12in/30cm pillow form

GAUGE
23 sts and 32 rows to 4in/10cm square
over St st using size 5 (3.75mm) needles.
24 sts and 32 rows to 4in/10cm square
over patterned St st using size 5
(3.75mm) needles, or size to obtain
correct gauge.

ABBREVIATIONS
See page 127.

NOTE
When working from chart, odd numbered
rows are purl rows and read from left to
right. Even numbered rows are knit rows
and read from right to left.
Use the Fair Isle method: strand the
yarns not in use across the wrong side
of work, weaving them under and over the
working yarn every 3 or 4 sts.

CHART A

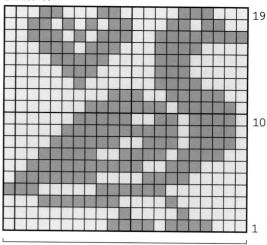

21-st patt rep

CHART B

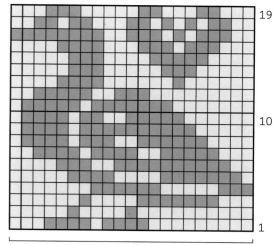

21-st patt rep

KEY
☐ Clay 177 (A)
▨ Avocado 161 (B)

FRONT

Using size 5 (3.75mm) needles and A, cast on 115 sts.

Beg with a k row, work in St st.

Work 4 rows.

Work in patt.

Row 1 K[3C, 3A] 19 times, k1C.

Row 2 P2C, [1A, 1C, 1A, 3C] 18 times, 1A, 1C, 1A, 2C.

Row 3 K1C, [3A, 3C] 19 times.

Rows 4 and 5 Using A, work in St st.

Work in patt from Chart A.

Row 6 P5A, [work across row 1 of 21-st patt rep] 5 times, p5A.

Row 7 K5A, [work across row 2 of 21-st patt rep] 5 times, k5A.

These 2 rows set Chart A with 5 sts in St st using A at sides.

Cont in patt to end of row 19.

Rows 25 and 26 Using A, work in St st.

Rows 27 to 31 As rows 1 to 5.

Work in patt from Chart B.

Row 32 P5A, [work across row 1 of 21-st patt rep] 5 times, p5A.

Row 33 K5A, [work across row 2 of 21-st patt rep] 5 times, k5A.

These 2 rows set Chart B with 5 sts in St st using A at sides.

Cont in patt to end of row 19.

Rows 51 and 52 Using A, work in St st.

Rows 53 to 57 As rows 1 to 5.

Work in patt from Chart A.

Row 58 P5A, [work across row 1 of 21-st patt rep] 5 times, p5A.

Row 59 K5A, [work across row 2 of 21-st patt rep] 5 times, k5A.

These 2 rows set Chart A with 5 sts in St st using A at sides.

Cont in patt to end of row 19.

Rows 77 and 78 Using A, work in St st.

Rows 79 to 81 As rows 1 to 3.

Rows 82 to 85 Using A, work in St st.

Using A, bind off.

BACK

Using size 5 (3.75mm) needles and A, cast on 110 sts.

Beg with a k row, work in St st.

Work 4 rows.

Work in stripes of ** 3 rows C, [3 rows A, 2 rows B] 4 times, 3 rows A.

Rep from ** twice more.

3 rows C, 4 rows A.

Using A, bind off.

FINISHING

With right sides together, sew back to front along three sides. Insert pillow form, join rem side.

paper boats pillow

FINISHED SIZE
19in/48cm by 11in/28cm to fit a 20in/50cm by 12in/30cm pillow form

YARN
Rowan *Felted Tweed*
2 x 1¾oz/191yd balls in each of Clay 177 (A), Seasalter 178 (B), and Cinnamon 175 (C)

NEEDLES
Pair of size 5 (3.75mm) knitting needles

EXTRAS
20in/50cm by 12in/30cm pillow form

GAUGE
23 sts and 32 rows to 4in/10cm square over St st using size 5 (3.75mm) needles. 24 sts and 32 rows to 4in/10cm square over patterned St st using size 5 (3.75mm) needles, or size to obtain correct gauge.

ABBREVIATIONS
See page 127.

NOTE
When working from chart, odd numbered rows are purl rows and read from left to right. Even numbered rows are knit rows and read from right to left.
Use the Fair Isle method: strand the yarns not in use across the wrong side of work, weaving them under and over the working yarn every 3 or 4 sts.

FRONT
Using size 5 (3.75mm) needles and A, cast on 115 sts.
Beg with a k row, work in St st.
Work 1 row.
Work in patt from Chart A.
Row 1 Work 3 sts before patt rep,
[work across 7-st patt rep] 16 times.
Row 2 [Work across 7-st patt rep]
16 times, work 3 sts after patt rep.
These 2 rows set the chart.
Work in patt to end of row 12.
Rows 13 to 36 Rep rows 1 to 12 twice more.
Work in patt from Chart B.
Row 37 Work 22 sts before patt rep,
[work across 46-st patt rep] twice,
work one st after patt rep.
Row 38 Work one st before patt rep,
[work across 46-st patt rep] twice,
work 22 sts after patt rep.
These 2 rows set the chart.
Work in patt to end of row 17.
Row 54 Using A, k to end.
Work in patt from Chart C.
Row 55 Work 3 sts before patt rep,
[work across 7-st patt rep] 16 times.
Row 56 [Work across 7-st patt rep]
16 times, patt 3 sts after patt rep.
These 2 rows set the chart.
Work in patt to end of row 12.
Rows 67 to 90 Rep rows 1 to 12 twice more.
Using A, bind off.

BACK
Using size 5 (3.75mm) needles and A, cast on 110 sts.
Beg with a k row, work in St st.
Work in stripes of 2 rows A,
[3 rows C, 3 rows A, 3 rows B, 3 rows A] twice, 3 rows C, 3 rows A, 3 rows B, 2 rows A, 4 rows B, 2 rows A, [2 rows B, 2 rows A] 3 times, [3 rows B, 3 rows A, 3 rows C, 3 rows A] twice, 3 rows B, 3 rows A, 3 rows C, 2 rows A.
Using A, bind off.

FINISHING
With right sides together, sew back to front along three sides. Insert pillow form, join rem side.

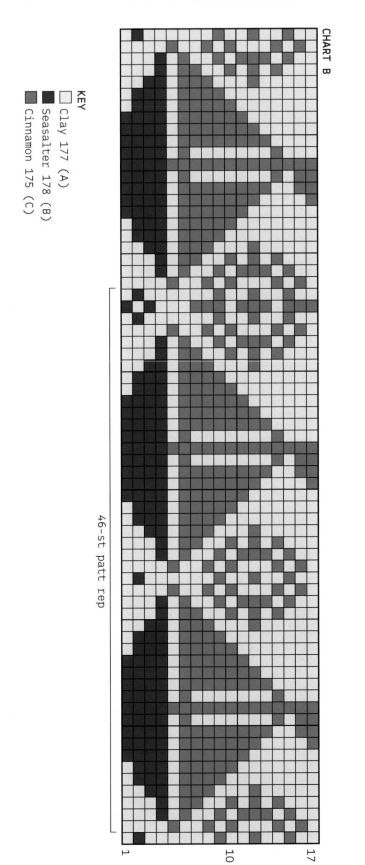

CHART B

KEY
☐ Clay 177 (A)
■ Seasalter 178 (B)
▨ Cinnamon 175 (C)

46-st patt rep

1   10   17

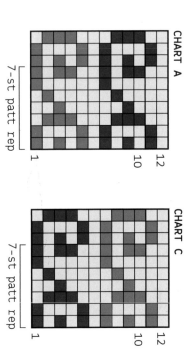

CHART A

7-st patt rep

1   10   12

CHART C

7-st patt rep

1   10   12

PAPER BOATS PILLOW 113

nordic garland

FINISHED SIZE
64in/165cm long

YARN
Rowan *Felted Tweed*
Small amount of Phantom 153 (A) for trunk
Oddments in an assortment of colors for tree (MC) and pattern (CC)
Approx ½oz of one color for i-cord

NEEDLES
Two double-pointed size 2 (2.75mm) knitting needles

EXTRAS
15 assorted buttons

ABBREVIATIONS
See page 127.

NOTE
When working from chart, odd numbered rows are knit rows and read from right to left. Even numbered rows are purl rows and read from left to right.
Use the Fair Isle method: strand the yarns not in use across the wrong side of work, weaving them under and over the working yarn every 2 or 3 sts.

GARTER ST NORDIC TREE
TRUNK
Using size 2 (2.75mm) needles and A, cast on 5 sts.
K10 rows.
Leave these sts on a spare needle.
MAIN PART
Using size 2 (2.75mm) needles, cast on 15 sts.
Row 1 (RS) K5, with wrong side of trunk to right side of work, [k1tog with one st from trunk] 5 times, k5.
Row 2 K to end.
Row 3 Skpo, k to last 2 sts, k2tog.

13 sts.
K 3 rows.
Rep the last 4 rows 5 times more. *3 sts.*
K3tog and leaving a long end, fasten off.

FAIR ISLE NORDIC TREE A
TRUNK
Using size 2 (2.75mm) needles and A, cast on 5 sts.
K 10 rows.
Leave these sts on a spare needle.
MAIN PART
Using size 2 (2.75mm) needles and MC, cast on 23 sts.
Row 1 (RS) K9, with wrong side of trunk to right side of work, [k1tog with one st from trunk] 5 times, k9.
Row 2 P to end.
Work in patt from row 3 of Chart A, shaping as shown.

FAIR ISLE NORDIC TREE B
TRUNK
Using size 2 (2.75mm) needles and A, cast on 7 sts.
K 10 rows.
Leave these sts on a spare needle.
MAIN PART
Using size 2 (2.75mm) needles and MC, cast on 27 sts.
Row 1 (RS) K10, with wrong side of trunk to right side of work, [k1tog with one st from trunk] 7 times, k10.
Row 2 P to end.
Work in patt from row 3 of Chart B, shaping as shown.

I-CORD
Using size 2 (2.75mm) needles, cast on 4 sts.
*K4, do not turn, slide sts back to other end of needle, bring yarn tightly across back of work; rep from * until i-cord measures 64in/165cm from beg. Bind off.

FINISHING

Arrange trees along i-cord 4¼in/11cm apart and secure top of tree to i-cord with a button.

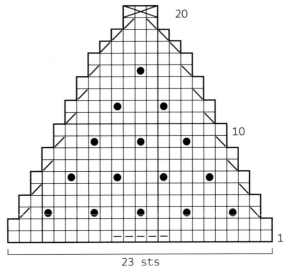

CHART A (Fairisle Nordic Tree A)

23 sts

KEY

- ☐ K on RS, P on WS in MC
- ⬛ K on RS, P on WS in CC
- ◪ k2tog on RS, p2tog on WS
- ◩ k2tog-tbl on RS, p2tog-tbl on WS
- ☒ k3tog on RS
- ⊟ graft on tree trunk

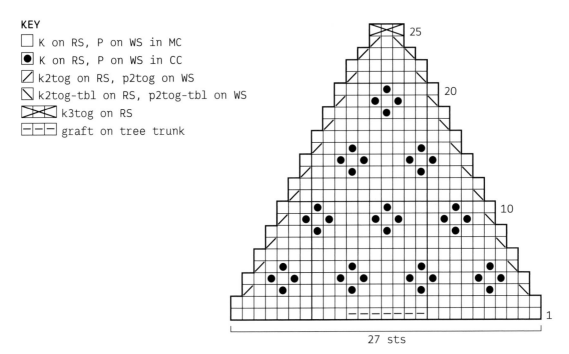

CHART B (Fairisle Nordic Tree B)

27 sts

nordic throw

FINISHED SIZE
Approx 31in/79cm by 42in/107cm

YARN
Rowan *Felted Tweed*
Approx 17½oz of assorted colors,
including Phantom 153 (A) for trunk
Each large square requires approx ½oz
of main color (MC)
We used 2 x 1¾oz/191yd balls of Mineral
181, for spots (CC) and edgings

NEEDLES
Pair each of size 2 (2.75mm) and size 5
(3.75mm) knitting needles
Size 3 (3.25mm) circular needle

GAUGE
23 sts and 32 rows to 4in/10cm square
over St st using size 5 (3.75mm) needles,
or size to obtain correct gauge.

ABBREVIATIONS
See page 127.

NOTE
When working from chart, odd numbered
rows are knit rows and read from right
to left. Even numbered rows are purl rows
and read from left to right.
Use the Fair Isle method: strand the
yarns not in use across the wrong side
of work, weaving them under and over the
working yarn every 3 or 4 sts.
You will need to make 35 motifs for the
Throw shown.

PLAIN SQUARES
Leaving a long end of approx 12in/30cm,
using size 5 (3.75mm) needles and color
of choice, cast on 37 sts.
Beg with a k row, work 44 rows in St st.
Bind off.

BIRD'S EYE SQUARE
Leaving a long end of approx 12in/30cm,
using size 5 (3.75mm) needles and color
of choice (MC), cast on 37 sts.
Row 1 K to end.
Row 2 P to end.
Row 3 K4MC, [1CC, 3MC] to last 5 sts, 1CC,
4MC.
Row 4 P to end.
Row 5 K to end.
Row 6 P2MC, [1CC, 3MC] to last 3 sts, 1CC,
2MC.
These 6 rows form the patt.
Work a further 38 rows, ending row 2.
Leaving a long end of approx 12in/30cm,
bind off.

GARTER ST NORDIC TREE
TRUNK
Leaving a long end of approx 8in/20cm,
using size 2 (2.75mm) needles and A,
cast on 5 sts.
K 10 rows.
Leave these sts on a spare needle.
MAIN PART
Leaving a long end of approx 12in/30cm,
using size 2 (2.75mm) needles and color
of choice (MC), cast on 15 sts.
Row 1 (RS) K5, with wrong side of trunk
to right side of work, [k1tog with one st
from trunk] 5 times, k5.
Row 2 K to end.
Row 3 Skpo, k to last 2 sts, k2tog. *13 sts.*
K 3 rows.
Rep the last 4 rows 5 times more. *3 sts.*
K3tog and leaving a long end, fasten off.

FAIR ISLE NORDIC TREE
TRUNK
Leaving a long end of approx 8in/20cm,
using size 2 (2.75mm) needles and A,
cast on 7 sts.
K 10 rows.
Leave these sts on a spare needle.

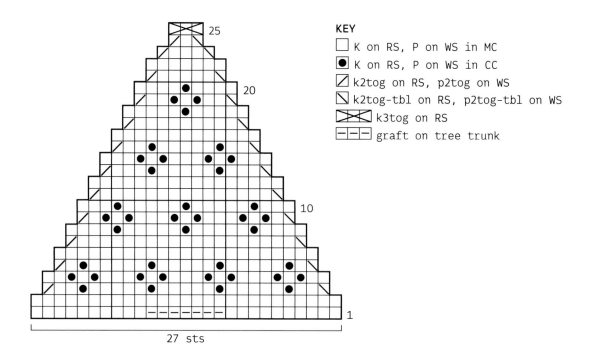

KEY

☐ K on RS, P on WS in MC

● K on RS, P on WS in CC

◢ k2tog on RS, p2tog on WS

◥ k2tog-tbl on RS, p2tog-tbl on WS

▨ k3tog on RS

⊟⊟ graft on tree trunk

MAIN PART

We created different size trees by using either size 2 (2.75mm) needles or size 5 (3.75mm) needles.

Leaving a long end of approx 12in/30cm, using size 2 (2.75mm) or size 5 (3.75mm) needles and color of choice (MC), cast on 27 sts.

Row 1 K10, with right side of trunk to wrong side of cast on row, [k1tog with 1 st from trunk] 7 times, k10.

Row 2 P to end.

Work in patt from row 3 of Chart, shaping as shown.

TOP EDGING

Sew trees to squares.

Join squares together to form a rectangle 5 squares wide by 7 squares deep and alternating motifs.

With right side facing, using size 3 (3.25mm) circular needle, pick up and k177 sts along bound-off edge.

Next row K to end.

Next row K1, m1, k to last st, m1, k1. *179 sts.*

Rep the last 2 rows twice more. *183 sts.* Bind off.

BOTTOM EDGING

With right side facing, using size 3 (3.25mm) circular needle, pick up and k177 sts along cast-on edge.

Work as given for top edging.

SIDE EDGINGS (both alike)

With right side facing, using circular needle, pick up and k196 sts along side edges.

Next row K to end.

Next row K1, m1, k to last st, m1, k1. *198 sts.*

Rep the last 2 rows twice more. *202 sts.* Bind off.

FINISHING

Join corners of edgings.

counting sheep throw

FINISHED SIZE
Approx 28in/70cm by 35½in/90cm

YARNS
Rowan *Felted Tweed*
3 x 1¾oz/191yd balls in each of Scree 165
(A) and Seafarer 170 (B)
1 x 1¾oz/191yd ball in Avocado 161 (C)

NEEDLES
Pair of size 5 (3.75mm) knitting needles
and size 3 (3.25mm) circular needle

GAUGE
24 sts and 28 rows to 4in/10cm square
over patterned St st using size 5
(3.75mm) needles, or size to obtain
correct gauge

ABBREVIATIONS
See also page 127.

NOTE
When working from chart, odd numbered
rows are knit rows and read from right
to left. Even numbered rows are purl
rows and read from left to right.
Use the Fair Isle method: strand the
yarns not in use across the wrong side
of work, weaving them under and over the
working yarn every 3 or 4 sts.

TO MAKE
RAM SQUARE (make 20)
Leaving a long end of approx 12in/30cm,
using size 5 (3.75mm) needles and A,
cast on 24 sts.
Beg with a k row. Work in St st from
chart for Ram Square to end of row 28.
Using A, bind off.

EWE SQUARE (make 12)
Leaving a long end of approx 12in/30cm,
using size 5 (3.75mm) needles and A,
cast on 24 sts.
Beg with a k row. Work in St st from
chart for Ewe Square to end of row 28.
Using A, bind off.

DOTS SQUARE (make 31)
Leaving a long end of approx 12in/30cm,
using size 5 (3.75mm) needles and B,
cast on 25 sts.
Beg with a k row. Work in St st from
chart for Dots Square to end of row 27.
Using B, bind off purlwise.

FINISHING
Using the photograph as a guide, join
squares together to form a rectangle
7 squares wide by 9 squares deep,
alternating motifs as shown, with a
Ram square at each corner of rectangle.
TOP EDGING
With right sides facing, using size 3
(3.25mm) circular needle and C, pick up
and k 161 sts along top edge (bound-off
edge) of Throw.
Next row K to end.
Next row K1, m1, k to last st, m1, k1.
Rep the last 2 rows twice more.
167 sts.
Bind off knitwise.
LOWER EDGING
With right sides facing, using size 3
(3.25mm) circular needle and C, pick up

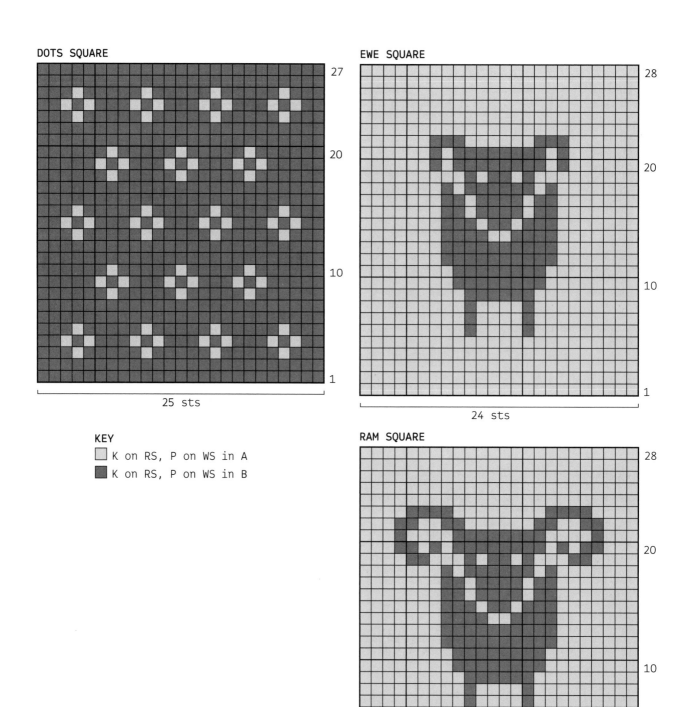

DOTS SQUARE

27
20
10
1

25 sts

EWE SQUARE

28
20
10
1

24 sts

RAM SQUARE

28
20
10
1

24 sts

KEY

☐ K on RS, P on WS in A
■ K on RS, P on WS in B

120 EASY FAIR ISLE KNITTING

and k161 sts along bottom
edge [cast-on edge] of
Throw.
Work as given for top
edging.
SIDE EDGINGS (both
alike)
With right sides facing,
using size 3 (3.25mm)
circular needle and C,
pick up and k201 sts along
side edges of Throw.
Next row K to end.
Next row K1, m1, k to last
st, m1, k1.
Rep the last 2 rows twice
more. *207 sts.*
Bind off knitwise.

FINISHING
Join corners of edgings.

little houses tablet cover

FINISHED SIZE
7in/18cm wide by 8½in/21.5cm deep

YARN
Rowan *Felted Tweed*
1 x 1¾oz/191yd ball in each of Granite
191 (A), Clay 177 (B), Ginger 154 (C),
Mineral 181 (D), Rage 150 (E), and Watery
152 (F)

NEEDLES
Pair each of size 3 (3.25mm) and size 5
(3.75mm) knitting needles

EXTRAS
2 buttons
Small piece of fabric 8in/20cm by
17¾in/45cm

GAUGE
23 sts and 32 rows to 4in/10cm square
over patterned St st using 3.75mm
(US 5) needles, or size to obtain correct
gauge.

ABBREVIATIONS
See page 127.

NOTE
When working from chart, odd numbered
rows are knit rows and read from right
to left. Even numbered rows are purl rows
and read from left to right.
Use the Fair Isle method: strand the
yarns not in use across the wrong side
of work, weaving them under and over the
working yarn every 3 or 4 sts.

TO MAKE
FIRST SIDE
Using size 5 (3.75mm) needles and A,
cast on 43 sts.
** Beg with a k row, work in St st and
patt from Chart.

Row 1 Using A, k to end.
Row 2 Work one st before patt rep,
[work across row 2 of 8-st patt rep]
5 times, work 2 sts after patt rep.
Row 3 Work 2 sts before patt rep,
[work across row 3 of 8-st patt rep]
5 times, work one st after patt rep.
Rows 2 and 3 set Chart.
Work in patt to end of row 32.
Then work rows 1 to 24 again.
Change to size 3 (3.25mm) needles.
Rib row 1 K1, [p1, k1] to end.
Rib row 2 P1, [k1, p1] to end.
These 2 rows form the rib **.
Work a further 10 rows.
Bind off in rib.
SECOND SIDE
Using size 5 (3.75mm) needles and A,
pick up and k43 sts along cast-on edge
of first side.
P 1 row.
Work as given for first side from ** to
**.
Work a further 2 rows.
Buttonhole row Rib 10, work 2tog, yrn,
rib 19, work 2tog, yrn, rib 10.
Work a further 7 rows.
Bind off in rib.

FINISHING
Allowing ½in/1cm for seams and using
knitted piece for template, cut out
lining. Join side seams. Join side seams
of knitted piece. With wrong sides
together place lining inside knitting.
Turn raw edge of fabric to wrong side
and slip st to first row of rib. Sew
on buttons to inside of first piece to
correspond with buttonholes.

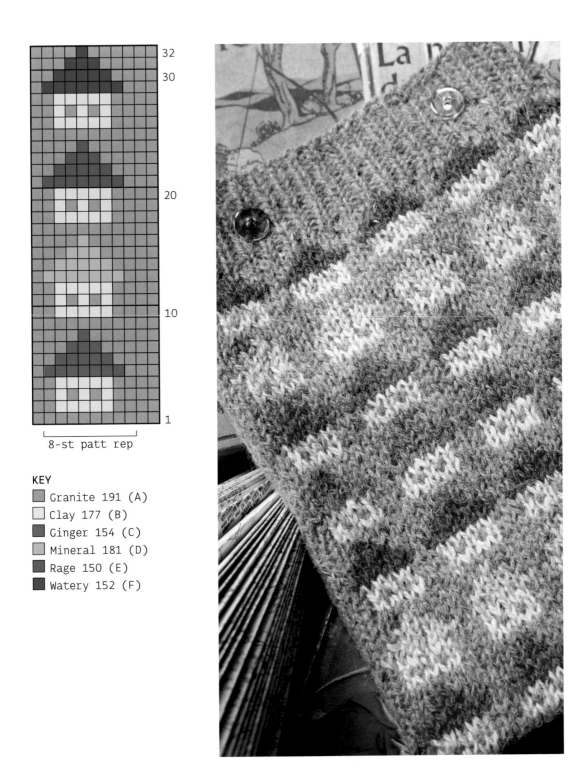

32
30

20

10

1

8-st patt rep

KEY
Granite 191 (A)
Clay 177 (B)
Ginger 154 (C)
Mineral 181 (D)
Rage 150 (E)
Watery 152 (F)

little houses i-phone cover

FINISHED SIZE
One size: 2¾in/7cm wide by 4¾in/12cm deep

YARN
Rowan *Felted Tweed*
1 x 1¾oz/191yd ball in Granite 191 (A)
Small amounts in each of Clay 177 (B),
Ginger 154 (C), Mineral 181 (D), Rage 150
(E), and Watery 152 (F)

NEEDLES
Pair each of size 3 (3.25mm) and size 5
(3.75mm) knitting needles

EXTRAS
One button
Small piece of fabric, 3½in/9cm by
10¼in/26cm

GAUGE
23 sts and 32 rows to 4in/10cm square
over patterned St st using size 5
(3.75mm) needles, or size to obtain
correct gauge.

ABBREVIATIONS
See page 127.

NOTE
When working from chart, odd numbered
rows are knit rows and read from right
to left. Even numbered rows are purl rows
and read from left to right.
Use the Fair Isle method: strand the
yarns not in use across the wrong side
of work, weaving them under and over the
working yarn every 3 or 4 sts.

TO MAKE
FIRST SIDE
Using size 5 (3.75mm) needles and A,
cast on 19 sts.
** Beg with a k row, work in St st and
patt from Chart.
Row 1 Using A, k to end.
Row 2 Work one st before patt rep,
[work across row 2 of 8-st patt rep]
twice, work 2 sts after patt rep.
Row 3 Work 2 sts before patt rep,
[work across row 3 of 8-st patt rep]
twice, work one st after patt rep.
Rows 2 and 3 set Chart.
Work in patt to end of row 32.
Change to size 3 (3.25mm) needles.
Rib row 1 K1, [p1, k1] to end.
Rib row 2 P1, [k1, p1] to end.
These 2 rows form the rib **.
Work a further 4 rows.
Bind off in rib.
SECOND SIDE
Using size 5 (3.75mm) needles and A,
pick up and k19 sts along cast-on edge
of first side.
P 1 row.
Work as given for first side from ** to **.
Buttonhole row Rib 8, work 2tog, yrn,
rib 9.
Work a further 3 rows.
Bind off in rib.

FINISHING
Allowing ½in/1cm for seams and using
knitted piece for template, cut out
lining. Join side seams. Join side seams
of knitted piece. With wrong sides
together, place lining inside knitting.
Turn raw edge of fabric to wrong side and
slip st to first row of rib. Sew on button
to inside of first piece to correspond
with buttonhole.

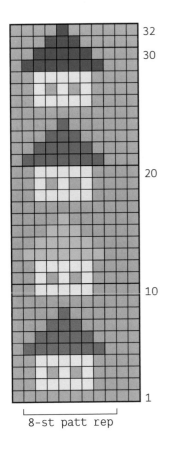

32
30

20

10

1

8-st patt rep

KEY
- ⬜ Granite 191 (A)
- ⬜ Clay 177 (B)
- 🟫 Ginger 154 (C)
- ⬜ Mineral 181 (D)
- 🟦 Rage 150 (E)
- 🟦 Watery 152 (F)

useful information

FAIR ISLE

When you are working a pattern with two (or more) repeating colors in the same row, you need to strand the yarn not in use behind the stitches being worked. This needs to be done with care, loosely enough to ensure that the strands not in work do not tighten and pucker the front of the knitting. To do this you need to treat the yarns not in use (known as floating yarns) as if they were one yarn and spreads the stitches as you work to their correct width to keep them elastic. If your pattern demands that the stranded (floating) yarns are carried across more than three stitches, it is wise each time you change colors to weave the new yarn color under and over the color yarn you are working (over the first time, under the second time, and so on). The alternating "under and over" movement helps to prevent the floating yarns from tangling by keeping them caught at the back of the work. If you tend to knit colorwork too tightly, increase your needle size for the colorwork section. If you make a minor mistake using the Fair Isle technique—say, just a single stitch—you can recreate it in the correct color using the duplicate stitch technique, in which you duplicate the stitch using a darning needle and the chosen color.

GAUGE

To check your gauge, knit a square in the pattern stitch and/or stockinette stitch of perhaps 5-10 more stitches and 5-10 more rows than those given in the gauge note. Press the finished square under a damp cloth and mark out the central 4in/10cm square with pins. If you have too many stitches to 4in/10cm, try again using thicker needles. If you have too few stitches to 4in/10cm, try again using finer needles.

CHART NOTES

Each square of the chart represents a stitch and each line of squares represents a row of knitting. When working from charts, read odd-numbered rows (K) from right to left and even numbered rows (P) from left to right, unless otherwise stated.

FINISHING METHODS
Pressing

Block out each piece of knitting by pinning it on a board to the correct measurements in the pattern. Then lightly press it according to the ball band instructions, omitting any ribbed areas. Take special care to press the edges as this makes sewing up easier and neater. Darn in all ends neatly along the selvedge edge or a color join, as appropriate.

Stitching seams

When you stitch the pieces together, remember to match any areas of color and texture carefully where they meet. After all the seams are complete, press the seams and hems.

ROWAN *FELTED TWEED*

A wool-alpaca-viscose mix (50 percent merino wool, 25 percent alpaca wool, 25 percent viscose); 1¾oz/50g (approx 191yd/175m) per ball. Recommended gauge: 22-24 sts and 30-32 rows to 4in/10cm in St st using size 5-6 (3.75-4mm) knitting needles.

ABBREVIATIONS

The knitting pattern abbreviations used in this book are as below.

alt	alternate
approx	approximately
beg	begin(s)(ning)
cm	centimeters
cont	continu(e)(ing)
CC	contrast color
dec	decreas(e)(ing)
foll(s)	follow(s)(ing)
g	gram
in	inch(es)
inc	increas(e)(ing)
k	knit
k2tog	knit next 2 sts together
MC	main color
mm	millimeters
m1	make one st by picking up horizontal loop before next st and knitting into back of it
0	no rows
oz	ounces
p	purl
patt	pattern
p2tog	purl next 2 sts together
rem	remain(s)(ing)
rep	repeat
RS	right side
rev St st	reverse stockinette stitch
skpo	sl 1, k1, pass slipped stitch over
sl 1	slip one st
sl 1pw	slip one st purlwise
st(s)	stitch(es)
St st	stockinette stitch (1 row knit, 1 row purl)
tbl	through back of loop(s)
tog	together
WS	wrong side
yd	yard(s)
yrn	yarn round needle
[ ]/*	repeat instructions within square brackets or between asterisks

acknowledgments

I would like to thank my usual team for their customary terrific work plus my niece, Harriet, and my friends Tonia and Dion for modeling with such panache. Grateful thanks, too, to the entire Rowan team for their ongoing support.

PUBLISHERS' ACKNOWLEDGMENTS
Many thanks to all involved in putting this book together, and to Martin and Mark for their hospitality during the photoshoot.

stockists

U.S.A.
Westminster Fibers Inc,
8 Shelter Drive, Greer
South Carolina 29650
www.westminsterfibers.com

U.K.
Rowan, Green Lane Mill,
Holmfirth,
West Yorkshire HD9 2DX
www.knitrowan.com

AUSTRALIA
Australian Country Spinners
Pty Ltd,
Melbourne, Victoria 3004
tkohut@auspinners.com.au

AUSTRIA
Coats Harlander Ges GmbH
1210 Vienna
www.coatscrafts.at

BELGIUM
See Germany

BULGARIA
Coats Bulgaria
BG-1784 Sofia
www.coastsbulgaria.bg

CANADA
Westminster Fibers Inc,
Vaughan, Ontario L4H 3M8
www.westminsterfibers.coom

CHINA
Coats Shanghai Ltd, Shanghai
victor.li@coats.com

CYPRUS
See Bulgaria

DENMARK
Coats Expotex AB, Dalsjöfors
info.dk@coats.com

FINLAND
Coats Opti Crafts Oy, Kerava
04200
www.coatscrafts.fi

FRANCE
www.coatscrafts.fr

GERMANY
Coats GmbH, Kenzingen 79341
www.coatsgmbh.de

GREECE
See Bulgaria

HONG KONG
East Unity Company Ltd,
Chai Wan
eastunityco@yahoo.com.hk

ICELAND
Rowan At Storkurinn,
Reykjavik 101
www.storkurinn.is

ITALY
Coats Cucirini srl, Milan
20126
www.coatscucirini.com

KOREA
Coats Korea Co. Lt,
Seoul 137-060
www.coatskorea.co.kr

LEBANON
y.knot, Saifi Village, Beirut
y.knot@cyberia.net.lb

LITHUANIA & RUSSIA
Coats Lietuva UAB,
Vilnius 09310
www.coatscrafts.lt

LUXEMBOURG
See Germany

NEW ZEALAND
ACS New Zealand,
Christchurch
64 3 323 6665

NORWAY
Coats Knappehuset AS,
Bergen 5873
kundeservice@coats.com

PORTUGAL
Coats & Clark,
Vila Nova de Gaia 4400
351 223 770700

SINGAPORE
Golden Dragon Store,
Singapore 058357
gdscraft@hotmail.com

SOUTH AFRICA
Arthur Bales Ltd,
Johannesburg 2195
arthurb@new.co.za

SPAIN
Coats Fabra,
Barcelona 08030
www.coatscrafts.es

SWEDEN
Coats Expotex AB
kundtjanst@coats.com

SWITZERLAND
Coats Stroppel AG,
Untersiggenthal 5417
www.coatscrafts.ch

TAIWAN
Cactus Quality Co Ltd,
Taiwan, R.O.C. 10084
00886-2-23656527

THAILAND
Global Wide Trading,
Bangkok 10310
global.wide@yahoo.com

For stockists in all other
countries please contact
Rowan for details